SCIENTIFIC ASPECTS OF
NATURE CONSERVATION
IN GREAT BRITAIN

:USSION

PHAM, F.R.S.

FFE

976

the
UNIVERSITY
of
GREENWICH

ETY

1977

Printed in Great Britain for the Royal Society
at the
University Press, Cambridge

ISBN 0 85403 089 1

First published in *Proceedings of the Royal Society of London*,
series B, volume 197 (no. 1126), pages 1–103

Published by the Royal Society
6 Carlton House Terrace, London SW1Y 5AG

PREFACE

The discussion on *The scientific aspects of nature conservation*, which this book reports, was held on 10 June 1976. It was the outcome of talks between representatives of the Royal Society, the Nature Conservancy Council and the Institute of Terrestrial Ecology. These were initiated after completion of the Nature Conservation Review in order to exchange views on the statement of policy in the Review. It was felt early in the talks that it would be valuable to arrange a meeting, open to all interested scientists and others, at which the scientific aspects of the policy and of its implementation might be discussed in public.

Nature conservation is of interest and concern to scientists for three main reasons, all of which were considered in contributions to the discussion. In the first place there is an important scientific content in most of the various meanings that have been attached to the term *nature conservation*. Secondly, arguments in favour of the acquisition and long-term protection of nature reserves are scientific, at least in part; and, thirdly, the management of nature reserves, so that they continue to fulfil the functions for which they were established, involves applying scientific knowledge and techniques and calls also for further scientific research where existing knowledge proves inadequate.

There are many today who, following the lead given by the American forester Gifford Pinchot in his book *The fight for conservation*, published in 1910, use the term 'conservation' to mean the development and wise use of material natural resources, including forests, agricultural land, water and minerals. This implies in particular maintaining the production of renewable resources at the highest possible level and demands scientific understanding both of basic biological processes and of the special requirements of those plants and animals that provide our utilizable crops. The desirability of nature conservation in this sense is generally agreed, especially in these times of increasing pressure on natural resources. Others, however, use the term in the different and narrower sense of setting certain areas aside as *nature reserves* in which as many as possible of our native plants and animals can be protected from extermination and where a representative set of plant communities, with their animal associates, can be preserved indefinitely for scientific study and research as well as for education and general enjoyment. Nature conservation is commonly used in a less precise way to cover any steps taken to ensure that wild plants and animals shall always remain conspicuous and delightful features of our surroundings. The term 'creative conservation' has recently been coined to cover the large-scale modifications of the landscape involved in the reclamation of land from the sea or of land once derelict because of mineral extraction or industrial development.

Professor Harley adopted the first of these definitions, but felt that the human needs to be satisfied by the wise use of land should include 'recreation, amenity and scientific study'. Dr Ratcliffe and others accepted the need for resource-conservation and the scientific effort and facilities it demands but emphasized the great importance of nature reserves on general scientific as well as on educational and amenity grounds. They pointed out that the U.K. contribution to the International Biological Programme depended heavily on nature reserves and other protected areas as sites for fundamental studies of the functioning of natural ecosystems that have an important bearing on problems of production. Reference was also made to other scientific reasons for the retention of substantial areas of nature reserves: that they protect rare species of plants and animals from extinction and so preserve them as future sources of scientific information and of genetic and experimental material, and that they provide suitable sites for monitoring environmental change such as might result from the pollution of air, land or water. To these was added the less exclusively scientific argument that both our natural and much of our man-modified vegetation, with its characteristic animals, are part of our national heritage which we should abandon no more lightly than our heritage of natural scenery or fine old buildings. Our fens and bogs, our heaths and moorlands, and also our woodlands of coppice-with-standards and our hedgerows, are parts of that environment of our forefathers that we wish to retain for study and enjoyment so that we can maintain a lively and informed sense of continuity with the past. That study will be in part scientific, but its aim will be historical understanding and intellectual satisfaction rather than the solution of current practical problems. Nature reserves alone can ensure the protection of this part of our heritage.

There are reasons for believing that even among scientists there is still too little awareness of the arguments in favour of nature reserves and it is most important that they should be understood and appraised. It is important because the benefits are mostly long-term and can therefore be thought less real than the obvious short-term advantages of using the lands of a nature reserve for producing food or timber, for extracting minerals or for siting a motorway. Arguments have been advanced against their establishment or retention, such as that research relevant to agricultural or forestry production is more suitably undertaken in the fields or plantations attached to the appropriate research institutions, and that rare plants and animals are more efficiently preserved in botanical or zoological gardens, than in nature reserves; and also that we do not need to conserve in this country communities and species that still flourish elsewhere. These arguments are misleadingly incomplete, especially in overlooking the all-important points that most species can be satisfactorily studied and conserved only as components of complex natural systems, and that such systems, once lost, are likely to be lost for ever. It is hoped that thoughtful readers of this book will come to a considered conclusion on the case for nature reserves and to a sympathetic understanding of the aims of the Nature Conservancy Council.

Lastly, the *management* of nature reserves is essentially a scientific matter and one of very considerable interest. Professor Pigott and Dr Dempster drew attention to possible differences of aim in managing reserves: whether, for example, to attempt to maintain the original system quite unchanged or to create something that might be better, as by being more diversified in habitat and richer in species. The achievement of different aims demands different management procedures, and these must be subjects for research in the best tradition of experimental science. The special problem of attempting to maintain unchanged the product of a type of land-use no longer practised demands an understanding of how the former stabilizing factors operated, as Professor Pigott pointed out. Dr Hellawell and Professor Bradshaw concentrated their attention on problems of change. They discussed the significance for management of various types of change inherent in ecosystems and of possible environmental change in the future, and also the measurement of change, whether short-term fluctuations or long-term trends.

The discussion ended with remarks by Mr R. E. Boote, director of the Nature Conservancy Council, in the course of which he stressed the need to use and extend our scientific understanding in order to retain what is best in our natural environment and to create new quality in it.

March 1977   A.R.C.

CONTENTS

PAGE

PREFACE   V

J. L. HARLEY, F.R.S.
The objectives of conservation   3
Discussion: V. C. Wynne-Edwards, S. M. Walters, D. A. Ratcliffe   9

D. A. RATCLIFFE
Nature conservation: aims, methods and achievements   11

J. M. HELLAWELL
Change in natural and managed ecosystems: detection, measurement and assessment   31
Discussion: J. D. Holloway   56

C. D. PIGOTT
The scientific basis of practical conservation: aims and methods of conservation   59
Discussion: S. M. Walters   68

J. P. DEMPSTER
The scientific basis of practical conservation: factors limiting the persistence of populations and communities of animals and plants   69

A. D. BRADSHAW
Conservation problems in the future   77

GENERAL DISCUSSION   97

R. E. BOOTE
Concluding remarks   101

Proc. R. Soc. Lond. B. **197**, 3–10 (1977)

Printed in Great Britain

The objectives of conservation

By J. L. Harley, F.R.S.

The wise use of land and the waters that it encloses is an important aim
that becomes especially pressing in thickly populated countries like Great
Britain. The pressures which result in changes in its use, its value to man,
and its biological potential are both natural and man-made and, although
irresistible, can be modified or reduced. Indeed, in Great Britain it
is fairly safe to assert, no area exists which is or has been unaffected by
human activity. Conservation has as its broad objective the wise use of
the whole area. In considering this general objective it is as unwise to
ignore the potential for productivity, whether biological or industrial, as
its value for recreation, amenity or scientific research or education. Nor
is the sentimental attachment of many of us to the traditional landscape
or uses of land a negligible consideration.

There are two primary scientific aspects of nature conservation. These
are the study of nature in the widest sense to provide knowledge and
skill for the conservation of nature, and the improvement and promotion
of natural knowledge that is of biological science itself.

The first of these scientific functions enables the elaboration of methods
to achieve the objectives of conservation whatever they may be and
allows the decision to be made whether these objectives are practicable.
But whether any given set of objectives should be sought if practicable, is
essentially a political decision.

The scientific researches undertaken for their own sake have as their
objective the resolution of problems concerning the ecology of organisms
and of ecosystems. From these too come a deeper understanding of
matters relevant to conservation. The effective and continued pursuit of
such researches requires selected areas to be set aside and controlled for
them.

The aims of conservation of nature are many and complex. There seems to be
great diversity in the stated aims of different people and different organizations.
Some on the one hand seem to wish to retain the countryside as it is or as it was in
their youth, essentially an area of pleasure. To the more serious an aim is to conserve natural communities and their species of plants and animals for scientific
study or for amenity, or recreation or as living museums of wildlife. To others
again the main aims are to use land wisely. That is both to ensure that it produces enough of its natural products of food, timber and minerals for human
needs, as well as the non-material benefits of recreation, amenity and scientific
study. I am of this last group.

However, whatever view is taken of its aims, conservation demands that some
land be allotted for purposes which are non-productive of material things. Land

may be so required totally, as in nature reserves or experimental areas; or in part, as in national parks, where constraints are put on the use or the changes of use of the land. Hence many acts of conservation must inevitably enter into competition for land with crop production for food, timber, pasture, mining quarrying, communications, living accommodation and recreation.

Such competition is inevitable and there is no escaping it, so it is worth while pausing to think about it. Our subject today concerns conservation in Britain, but production of food, wood and other materials from land concerns the whole world. There is a world shortage of food now, and a world timber shortage is expected in the next 25–30 years. We have to accept, therefore, that any act of conservation that has as a consequence reduced biological production in this country would appear to mean either that we reduce our present standards of life, or that we parasitize further a world of shortages, or that we must reduce our population.

But does it inevitably mean one of these three things? There is a further possibility and that is that the production per unit area of the cropped land must be increased.

The fundamental and immediate effort of conservation in my view must be in elaboration of methods of increased efficiency of crop production; not in the examination of details of nutrient cycling of ecosystems, or the habitat requirements of rare plants, although these activities have their importance. In so far as their efforts concentrate upon increased production per unit area and decreased fossil energy input per tonne of crop, the researches of such bodies as the Agricultural Research Council are more fundamental to conservation than those of many ecologically orientated research bodies.

There has been a continued upward trend of production per hectare in agriculture in Britain and in U.S.A. since 1947. It is this kind of increased production per unit area which makes conservation of nature even possible to contemplate.

In my view this competition between conservation for non-material benefits and for scientific research on the one hand and the use of land for production on the other will always exist. It is for politicians to resolve it and for scientists, especially biologists, to provide them with sound advice – especially advice as to how ecological researches or agricultural or silvicultural researches may improve productivity in the long term and make conservation of non-material benefits possible. I would like to emphasize further the point that problems concerning themselves with increased production and efficient use of land for crops may include as important components direct conservation of ecosystems and environments.

The speakers that follow me will be making use of British examples of scientific conservation to illustrate their points, so I will not steal their thunder, but draw my examples from the world at large. My first example concerns the work that my colleagues are doing in the Unit of Tropical Silviculture in Oxford. In our Tropical Pines Project we have several clear objectives. First, to provide fast-growing timber trees for lowland tropical areas which may be grown on cut-over or derelict land. These will provide a source of timber and forest products and so reduce the pressure on natural tropical forests for firewood and constructional material. To bring this about we are collecting as wide a range as possible of ecological (perhaps genetic) variants of Central American pines, such as *P. caribaea* and *P. oocarpa*. The seeds collected are being stored and distributed for trials in 40 or more countries. Many of the ecotypes are found already to be in danger of destruction in their native areas, and when this is so the matter is being brought to the notice of the countries in which it is taking place, and indeed our collections themselves are an important step in their conservation to be followed by their growth in trials or in conservation areas. Implicit in the collection of variants is an intraspecific taxonomic appraisal of the species and a consequent spin off of taxonomic and ecological problems.

Of course this project is only some seven or so years old but it is going ahead in the foreseeable future and it is an example where production considerations are basic to efficient and effective conservation. The project has been directly financed mainly by O.D.M. with help for a period from F.A.O. But the invisible input far exceeds the direct finance because of the contributions in scientific work by the 40 or so countries which are involved in the trials. As a corollary to this set of problems we are now joining in with research on the structure and regeneration of natural tropical high forest ecosystems which we are helping to conserve.

This example is not by any means unique in world forestry. The New Zealand Beech Scheme (Kirkland & Johns 1973; Thompson 1973) which has been criticized, often unfairly, as destructive by extremists is potentially a similar kind of conservation exercise in a country where the export of wood chips and pulp and the reduction of unemployment might be politically and economically expedient. As far as I have been able to judge it should be possible to combine conservation of *Nothofagus* ecosystems, the conservation of montane soils and water catchment areas, the conservation of amenities and the provision of recreational areas with efficient wood production and processing if the diverse interests combine to refine and perfect the plan as it is now.

For me the danger of this plan lies not in the plan itself but in the frailty of the human species. The introduction of *Pinus radiata* and *Eucalyptus* spp. into certain areas is a regrettable necessity to make the plan viable in terms of production. It requires honest self-discipline to limit the areas given to these exotics to the minimum which is essential now and in the future. The risk is that their production will be so much greater than the natural *Nothofagus* that there will be always pressure to extend their areas.

The application of these ideas to conservation in Britain is possible. It requires, however, a change of outlook both of us all and of many ecological scientists. We have for too long regarded ourselves as drawing our food and raw materials from the whole world as of right. We have still the idea that we can buy what we want. But if we use our land for amenity, recreation or pleasure, if we waste it by inefficient biological production or building, we parasitize the rest of the world for the products of land. We must realize that efficient production and conservation must go hand in hand.

For the ecologist a change of outlook is also necessary. We must accept that you cannot measure good or bad with a metre rule nor even with a flame photometer nor Geiger counter, and the scientist is no better at judging good from bad than the next man. The work of the ecologist is to carry out scientific investigation, to predict what changes will take place in the distribution of organisms in the survival of species or structure of ecosystems if this or that constraint is put upon them. Only by scientific work of this kind with no overtones of good or bad or quality judgements can conservation be furthered by ecologists as such.

I make no apologies for these introductory remarks because our subject of conservation in Britain is in a real sense an abstraction; it is an integral part of conservation in the whole world and to pursue it we must be aware of its wider non-parochial repercussions. It seems to me that in the narrower view of nature conservation we are seeking to ensure the existence for the future of living species in their natural or semi-natural ecosystems. The purposes of these objectives of conservation are to provide a desirable backcloth for the human stage and also amenity and recreation. We are seeking to conserve living species with their full range of genetic variation, including useful species and species whose use to man may be negligible or yet unknown. Implicit in the conservation of species is the conservation of the living systems, the ecosystems, of which these species are a part, because in this way their variation, evolution and activities can also be conserved.

All these activities require far more ecological knowledge and ecological insight than we at present possess. And we can classify the efforts required of scientists under the now conventional headings of strategic and fundamental research. The strategic researches involve in particular problems of protection and maintenance of areas or biological systems chosen for conservation. The fundamental researches involve the study and explanation of the range of variability of species, their environmental demands, their interaction with one another and the structure and physiology of the ecosystems which they together comprise. The carrying out of such research requires precise objectives of conservation of each particular area to be clear and we can discern two broad kinds of objective. There is the objective to conserve an ecological situation as it exists and there is then the objective to conserve an ecological area for scientific investigation. These objectives are different, although they may at times be combined.

The first consideration of importance in the conservation of an ecosystem as it exists is to determine its status, that is the factors which tend to maintain it in its present state and those which promote most rapidly its change. I think that to me the most enlightening contribution to the consideration of this general problem was Dr A. S. Watts's presidential address to the Ecological Society in 1947 'Pattern and process in the plant community'. This paper graphically illustrated a well known but inadequately appreciated feature of ecosystems that they are compounded of parts, each of which is not stable but passing through a series of changes dependent on growth, senescence and regeneration of the plants of which it is compounded and with these changes the consequent changes in the dependent animals. This thesis emphasizes that there must in theory be a minimum area which can be maintained in constant structure. The concept of such a minimum area is founded on probability. The probability that calamities such as flooding, wind and so on are rare. If we take these relative improbabilities into account our required area is increased. The impact of such infrequent but highly influential factors has been emphasized especially in the study of forest communities, as for instance by Dr T. C. Whitmore in the Solomons (Whitmore 1974), but it is of importance in many types of community.

However, there is yet a further complicating feature; this is the recognition of the relationship of an ecosystem to the surrounding pattern of other such systems. I can illustrate what I have in mind by the example of the raised bog. Here we have a pattern of ecological communities exactly arranged and compounded to give a total ecosystem whose structure depends on their spatial and lateral arrangement in the context of topography. The central raised area of ombrogenous peat is dependent on the existence of the less acid lag which causes any drainage water containing bases to be carried away without affecting the central acid region. The change in structure from down slope to up slope in the central peat area is a change from Calluna-dominated relatively static conditions to Sphagnum-dominated peat-growth conditions which depend upon a maintained high acid water level on the up slope side. The whole could be conserved but the parts cannot really exist without the whole. Such consideration applies to many ecosystems.

I stress these elementary examples to emphasize that conservation of the *status quo* demands a detailed knowledge of the ecological situation and usually even now considerable research in any particular case.

Ecological research, research upon the interaction of organisms and their effects upon one another requires areas, open-air laboratories, where observations can be made and experiments done. In experimental work, rather than pure observation, the ecologist may destroy his experimental materials as surely as does a physiologist or biochemist. Consequently areas conserved for ecological research are of two kinds; those carefully managed or controlled so that they stay stable or undergo change while being observed and recorded by ecologists making the minimum disturbance; then there are those areas in which ecosystems are disturbed, or to use modern jargon perturbed, or subjected to destructive sampling for experimental purposes. Of course these two kinds of activity are not entirely separate; sampling which may be destructive on a small scale community may be irrelevant to the scale of a large ecosystem. Nor is it that ecological work requires natural or semi-natural diverse systems. Much can be learned from artificial situations. Let me stress the advantages of the uniformity of a perennial crop like a forest plantation for the initial studies of complex problems. Their value has been demonstrated extremely well by Ovington (1962), for instance, in his widely quoted work on nutrient cycling which started many more observers on more difficult aspects of this subject. In a similar way my colleague, Mr P. F. Entwistle, and his friends in the Unit of Invertebrate Virology are using the uniformity of spruce plantations in Wales to study the movement and spread of pathogens in a population of insects. The nuclear polyhedrosis virus of the spruce saw fly has provided an example for study not only of the spread of the pathogen but also its effect on the host population and on the populations of predators and food plants of that host. A study both of direct ecological and economic relevance. The complexity of a natural community would impose almost insuperable complications until the initial work has been done.

When areas or ecosystems are set aside for ecological research the objectives for their use must be clear and must be planned in great detail. The planning of the way of using natural experimental areas must in the long run be as detailed as that of the experimental plans at Rothamsted or any other field station. If it is not, complicated errors of interpretation will result and great confusions will be caused. Indeed, over and above curiosity about ecological problems are more mundane ecological problems of land use directly and intensely relevant to pure research.

Lastly I am going the full cycle, like all good biological processes, from respiratory metabolism to regeneration of ecosystems, and I ask the question, can we increase the ecological productivity of land like we can increase the agricultural productivity?

Of course we can. There are great and interesting problems concerning the ecology of destroyed and derelict land, pit heaps, slag heaps, mining spoil, sand and gravel quarries and the like. Here there are real problems of conservation, and there are problems of resistance of organisms to toxic compounds in the soil and its genetic variation. If such areas of land can be used on a larger scale than they are now for experimentation and following that for amenity, recreation, pleasure and wildlife, they increase the available space and reduce the competition between food and essential production and conservational ecology.

Let me draw your attention to one example of many experiments going on at the moment. The work of Chadwick (1973 a, b) on pit heaps and mining spoil. The experimental work of his group has included research on the weathering of soil materials, leaching of substances and toxic chemicals, the origins of soil acidity, the tolerance of species and their genotypes to soil environments. Recreation, amenity and pleasant areas have been created out of a mess as a result of their work.

In this talk I have tried to emphasize that conservation of nature is a large and extensive enterprise. It is an international or global enterprise and it has to be paid for. It is an activity not to be entered upon with prejudice or emotion but coolly and scientifically. It requires a consideration both of the physical needs of man as well as his intellectual needs.

In conclusion let me say that I am aware that I might be criticized because I have stressed material things and that conservation should consider the beauty of the countryside. Some think that wilderness is essential to this beauty. But aesthetic uplift may sometimes be given by a countryside where every possible square centimetre is given to production and only the rocks are left untouched.

REFERENCES (Harley)

Chadwick, M. J. 1973 *a* Methods of assessment of acid colliery spoil as a medium for plant growth. In *Ecology and reclamation of devastated land* (eds R. J. Hutnik & G. Davis), vol. 1, pp. 81–90. New York: Gordon & Breach.

Chadwick, M. J. 1973 *b* Amendment trials of coal spoil in the North of England. In *Ecology and reclamation of devastated land* (eds R. J. Hutnik & G. Davis), vol. 2, pp. 175–186. New York: Gordon & Breach.

Entwistle, P. K. 1971 Possibility of control of a British outbreak of spruce sawfly by a virus disease. *Br. Insectic. Fungic. Conf.*, pp. 475–479.

Kirkland, A. & Johns, J. H. 1973 *Beech forests*. N.Z. Forest Service, Wellington, New Zealand, p. 48.

Ovington, J. D. 1962 Quantitative ecology and the woodland ecosystem concept. *Adv. Ecol. Res.* 1, 103–192.

Thompson, A. P. 1973 Government approval of West Coast and Southland beech forest utilization proposals. N.Z. Forest Service, Wellington, New Zealand, p. 16.

Watt, A. S. 1947 Pattern and process in the plant community. *J. Ecol.* 35, 1–22.

Whitmore, T. C. 1974 Change with time and role of cyclones in Tropical Rain Forest on Kolombangara in Solomon Islands. *Inst. Pap. Common. For. Inst.*

Discussion

V. C. WYNNE-EDWARDS (*Department of Zoology, University of Aberdeen*). Professor Harley observed that 'the ecologist must not introduce ideas of good or bad into his research'. I would suggest that in one important respect this statement needs to be qualified.

I do of course agree that scientists must seek and tell the truth objectively, resisting the temptation to bend their findings to support preconceived theories or dogmas. Nevertheless in applied science of every kind, whether in industry, engineering, medicine, agriculture or nature conservation, the researcher sets out to obtain useful results, and what is useful is by definition also good. Useful and good are not absolute qualities: to a greater or lesser extent they depend on value judgements or untested assumptions, or both. Often in the applied science of nature conservation the ecologist is far better equipped than anyone else to make the initial value judgements, and thus enable scientific effort to be applied. If he does not decide for himself what is useful and ought to be done, then conservation will be unsuccessful or will go by default.

It seems to me not only quite proper, but in fact vital, that the ecologist should make such judgements, and when necessary enter the political arena to obtain support for acting upon them. As long as his motives are disinterested and not swayed by self-interest, the sense of mission which inspires his judgements and promotes his efforts is, in my view, entirely laudable. It need not in any way interfere with his objectivity in research, or with his integrity as a scientist.

S. M. WALTERS (*University Botanic Gardens, Cambridge*). I cannot agree that as scientists we are not concerned with ethical questions. In practice we are all both scientists and citizens, and it is impossible, even if it were desirable, for us to dissociate ourselves from the responsibility of making value judgements. After all, what we investigate in our scientific research involves a value judgement, and we are all here today, I hope and assume, because we are in various ways *concerned* about the conservation of nature. This is good. The problems we face are both urgent and complex. Realistically, I am forced to conclude that, unless something unexpectedly good happens, we shall lose in the next decade perhaps half to three quarters of the remaining 3500 or so Sites of Special Scientific Interest in Great Britain. The official bodies concerned have not, apparently, the desire or the resources to prevent it, and the voluntary organizations are not powerful or wealthy enough. It we really care, we can conserve nature, but we shall only do it by caring enough and giving the task priority in time, energy and money.

D. A. RATCLIFFE (*Nature Conservency Council, London*). In reply to a question about the attitudes of farmers to nature conservation: This question connects with the point which Professor Harley made about the value to nature conservation of improvements in agricultural efficiency. There is a great deal of goodwill towards nature conservation within the farming community but, in our free enterprise society, each farmer is dominated by his own personal economics, and it is no use asking him to take measures which are financially disadvantageous to him unless (*a*) he is extremely wealthy, (*b*) he receives adequate compensation, or (*c*) all other farmers are prepared to do the same. The theoretical advantage of an efficient agricultural system which would allow the setting aside of land for nature conservation, instead of exploiting it fully for farming, could only work if there were truly centralized planning control, and this we do not have. If farmers are shown the way to increase the production from their land, they will all wish to take advantage of this.

Proc. R. Soc. Lond. B. **197**, 11–29 (1977)

Printed in Great Britain

Nature conservation: aims, methods and achievements

By D. A. Ratcliffe

The Nature Conservancy Council, London

Nature conservation aims to safeguard in perpetuity the essential subjects of study for natural scientists interested in the biota and the physical features of this country. Its basic strategy is to promote measures which minimize environmental damage resulting from human activities, following an evaluation of intrinsic importance of the features concerned and their vulnerability to disturbance. The establishment of nature reserves makes it possible to safeguard the most important areas of land and water by appropriate management programmes, and there are at present 150 National Nature Reserves, covering *ca.* 120 000 ha. Lesser categories of safeguard include Sites of Special Scientific Interest, of which 3500 have been notified. Conservation outside these protected areas is achieved by the provision of advice on land use and planning, by publicity and education and by legislation. The efficacy of these measures depends on adequate scientific information from surveys, recurrent observations and ecological research. This necessitates a considerable research effort yielding in return the substantial advances in basic ecological understanding which are an ultimate aim of nature conservation.

INTRODUCTION

Nature conservation has come to mean different things to different people, and any discussions of its aims has to identify the particular viewpoint on which these are based. My viewpoint is that of a member of staff of the official organization for nature conservation in Great Britain, concerned to summarize the course which policy and practice have taken within the body, but in relation to parallel developments outside.

Some people are able to see the conservation of nature as a unity, in which all natural resources are, or should be, managed in an integrated and harmonious way, to the betterment of both the material and spiritual well-being of mankind. A basic dichotomy of attitude has, however, arisen between those wishing to conserve wildlife and physical features for aesthetic and intellectual reasons, and those motivated by concern for improvement of the material and economic conditions of humanity through better utilization of natural resources.

The nature conservation movement is now identified most closely with the first concern, and I believe this to be true also of the part played by the official organization. It is therefore taken as the premise underlying this essay.

HISTORICAL DEVELOPMENTS

Nature conservation as an endeavour driven by aesthetic and intellectual purpose has, however, evolved gradually from an earlier concern over the maintenance of natural resources for more practical and economic reasons. Nicholson (1970) has reviewed the growth of the movement and pointed out that its modern development owes most to Britain and North America. In the United States, nature conservation began as the defence of wilderness, through the writings and proselytizings of leading figures such as Ralph Emerson, Henry Thoreau, John Muir, Theodore Roosevelt and Aldo Leopold. This has been expressed especially in the National Parks and National Wilderness Preservation Systems. Hand-in-hand there developed concern and action for the conservation of the great national resources of soil, water, forests and game. In Britain, with its environment so largely moulded by centuries of human activity, nature conservation became more specifically concerned in early days with wildlife, especially birds and rare Lepidoptera. The writings of W. H. Hudson made considerable impact, but we had rather fewer philosopher-naturalists over here, and the practical conservation measures were initiated mostly by certain more enlightened members of an otherwise hardened generation of specimen collectors. General bird protection measures were an early step, with the creation in 1889 of a Society for the Protection of Birds; and the foundation in 1895 of the National Trust for Places of Historic Interest or Natural Beauty marked a beginning to the protection of certain areas important for their wildlife. In 1912 Charles Rothschild led the setting-up of the Society for the Promotion of Nature Reserves, which acquired Woodwalton Fen, Huntingdonshire, to protect and manage the reintroduced population of the large copper butterfly *Lycaena dispar* which had become extinct in 1865 through the draining of the East Anglian Fenland.

Nature conservation in Britain made its biggest advance – quite surprisingly – during World War II, when leading ecologists, naturalists and other concerned people came together and through various committees presented views on the requirements for this aspect of post-war reconstruction. The Royal Society itself set up one of these committees, but the definition of a corporate philosophy and the translation of this into a policy for action was expressed most effectively by the Wild Life Conservation Special Committee (England and Wales). Their report *The conservation of nature in England and Wales* (Cmd 7122) was published as a Government White Paper and recommended the setting up of an official body for nature conservation, which it called *The Biological Service*. A parallel Scottish Wildlife Conservation Committee worked with a Scottish National Parks Committee in producing two complementary but shorter reports (Cmds 7235 and 7814) which endorsed the above recommendation.

Cmd 7122 contained a remarkable distillation of wisdom and foresight, and managed to convey a holistic conception of nature conservation as a single great endeavour, with both objectives and methods resting on a firm foundation of science. Events since its publication in 1947 have given substance to the earlier vision in many respects, but not in all. The recommended official body for nature conservation was established in 1949 as the Nature Conservancy, with responsibility for physical as well as biological features, and naturally took Cmd 7122 as its blueprint for action. The body itself has been subject to the organizational vicissitudes which tend to beset Government departments, culminating in 1973 in the splitting of the conservation and research functions. This involved the creation of two new and quite separate organizations, the Nature Conservancy Council and the Institute of Terrestrial Ecology, which were intended to maintain a close connection through a customer-contractor relationship for conservation research, in keeping with contemporary Government thinking on arrangements for applied research and development.

The last 30 years have also been marked by a tremendous growth of the non-official movement for nature conservation, during which the amateur and voluntary sector has increased in size and coordination. In particular, the Royal Society for the Protection of Birds; the Society for the Promotion of Nature Reserves, working through the County Naturalists' Trusts; the British Trust for Ornithology; the Wildfowl Trust; and the Field Studies Council have made enormous contributions to the total effort. Parallel concern for amenity and recreational values has been expressed in the formation of the two Countryside Commissions whose work, along with that of the two expanding National Trusts, has complemented and enhanced the nature conservation effort. Finally, there has been increasing acceptance by land users in general, including private individuals, industrial concerns and public bodies, of their responsibilities for nature conservation.

I wish now to look at what has happened during the last 30 years, in terms of the goals that have been set, the ways in which they have been pursued, and the results by which we can judge their success or lack of it.

NATURE CONSERVATION VALUE

It is necessary to consider briefly some of the more specific tenets which underlie the objectives of nature conservation, since a certain degree of misunderstanding about these has arisen. Scientists had a large part in the writing of Cmd 7122 and it is only natural that they placed great emphasis on the importance of the circular relationship between nature conservation and science. Nature conservation was seen as an activity aimed especially at fostering science, while also being partly dependent for its methods and success on research intended to provide further information and insight. Para. 50 contains an especially lucid exposition of these matters, in terms of promoting work in a whole range of scientific sub-disciplines, in providing facilities for field experimentation and in conducting ecological studies to resolve management problems. The terms 'scientific interest' or 'scientific importance' were freely used and became adopted in the language of legislation.

More recently they have been questioned increasingly as woolly if not pretentious terms rather than meaningful expressions of real values. Nature conservation to-day is seen as serving a far wider spectrum of human concern than science and scientists. It has, I believe, become much more heavily weighted towards the opposite pole of this spectrum, the aesthetic/amenity end. There would thus be greater honesty in substituting the more cumbersome term 'nature conservation value' for 'scientific interest (or importance)'. This is still a hopelessly under-defined term, but it does at least make the important connotation of nature con-servation as something concerned with value judgements, and hence subjectivity, whereas the word scientific has strong implications for objectivity. Nature con-servation is underlain by layers of value judgement, whereas science finds such things uncomfortable. The judgements themselves tend to express consensus, or perhaps sometimes compromise, views on what is desirable or important about the state of nature over an extremely wide field of interest.

The components of the natural world are evaluated mainly according to their relative importance to man. Sometimes it is possible to discern grades of what might be termed intrinsic importance, as between the dominants of a community and its subsidiary species. The tree species which dominate a particular woodland have more influence on the total character of the ecosystem than do herbaceous plants of the field layer. Similarly, in Britain, herbivorous members of an animal community such as the rabbit *Oryctolagus cuniculus* and short-tailed field vole *Microtus agrestis* have particular importance in determining presence and abund-ance of large predators, as well as in influencing the floristic composition of their habitat. On the whole, though, species and their aggregations as communities are valued according to a more specifically human viewpoint of either utility (or, conversely, harmfulness), aesthetic appeal, or scientific interest. Physical features are seen in a similar light. There is also a tacit rather than explicit recognition that wildlife values are related to the numbers of people concerned – the scale of public interest – so that 'popular' groups tend to be regarded as the most important. Birds in general are highly valued, but within the much larger Order of insects, only the butterflies and moths have a similar appeal.

The question of values is further complicated by that of *priorities* when con-servation action is required. Wildlife conservation in Britain could be likened to a defensive rearguard action against the inexorable advance of overwhelmingly superior forces. This may seem an over-dramatic simile, but the accepted strategy for nature conservation operates as though it were largely true. It assumes that, while there are wide differences in the importance of the features at risk, those which are likely to suffer the greatest or most rapid loss, and which are at the same time the most difficult to restore once lost, have prior claims for defensive action. There is no point in worrying over species which are flourishing or habitats which are actually being created extensively, such as exotic conifer forests; but every reason to make efforts to save threatened rare species and vanishing types of habi-tat. The goal is to maintain the national diversity of both species and habitats, or at least to minimize the losses which are inevitable. The more specific values of size of area or populations, diversity, naturalness, rarity and fragility, as applied to both ecosystems and species, are to a considerable extent related to this concept of irreplaceability or chances of survival. They thus have a built-in component of evaluation concerned with urgency for action as well as intrinsic merits, and they tend to highlight the exceptional rather than the ordinary.

This is a point on which some scientists appear to misunderstand the nature conservation requirements. It is sometimes said that the methods used, as in survey, are insufficiently objective to be valid, but this assumes that orthodox sampling theory is applicable to the subjects under investigation. The phenomena with which nature conservation deals are not neutral and objective, but have already had a scale of values imposed upon them – especially those connected with fragility and priority. They are thus not consonant with concepts of probability and the normal distribution of variation. On the contrary, they are by definition subjective and heavily biased. This is not to deny that methodological rigour is important to the solution of nature conservation problems; it is simply to ask that the suit be cut according to the cloth, and to require choice of methods which are appropriate both to the objectives and the limitations of the data or their collection. Conversely, nature conservation should not pretend to be more scientific than it ever can be. It is an activity which attempts to integrate a wide range of need and viewpoint, of which science is only one aspect. It acts in part as a handmaiden to science, drawing on scientific methods as appropriate to solve specific problems, but with the objective of safeguarding in perpetuity the essential subjects of study for natural scientists interested in the biota and the physical features of this country.

In summary, the objectives of nature conservation in Great Britain could be expressed as the maintenance of as much as possible of the wild fauna and flora, both as individual species and communities, and of the natural physical features; for the purposes of scientific study, education, aesthetic enjoyment and economic use. This interpretation allows that enhancement by immigration or by genetic divergence and decline or exinction through 'natural' causes are acceptable as a normal part of evolution; and that potential for the future is maintained to cope with shift in emphasis within the range of purpose. It perhaps does not express the view held by many people that nature conservation should be part of a civilized ethic whereby humanity establishes a more harmonious relationship within the global ecosystem, and that there should be less preoccupation with the uses to which nature can be put.

THE METHODS OF NATURE CONSERVATION

From its earliest days, the practice of nature conservation has relied on a two-pronged approach. First is the strict protection and management of the most important areas of land or water, originally to protect threatened species, but now more usually to conserve whole assemblages of plants and animals as well as rarities; and including also a range of important geological and physiographic features whose continued existence could not otherwise be taken for granted. The second approach is by influencing, through a broad advisory role, the attitudes and actions of people who collectively control or affect the nature conservation resource through the rest of the country outside the nature reserves. These include especially the owners and occupiers of land, the planners, the developers and exploiters of natural resources, and the recreation-seeking public. In short, the environmental users are the target for a programme which seeks to educate them to their responsibilities and to infuse both ecological thinking and the sense of need for conservation of renewable resources into their activities.

Both elements of this overall programme involve close cooperation with the voluntary bodies for nature conservation and liaison with organizations, both official and other, whose remit requires that they take account of nature conservation. Both also require the support of research aimed at expanding knowledge and understanding of the nature conservation resource.

The safeguarding of important areas

The pre-1940 selection of nature reserves in Britain was small and somewhat haphazard in choice, and a primary concern of the Wild Life Conservation Special Committee was to identify an adequate list of areas important for their biological and physical features which should be established as National Nature Reserves. For England and Wales Cmd 7122 proposed 73 National Nature Reserves, of which 13 were considered to be already in safe keeping and 42 geological monuments. In addition, there were proposals for 52 Conservation Areas and 35 Scientific Areas within National Parks and Conservation Areas or, in some cases, coterminous with the latter. In addition, there was a recommendation for the scheduling of an unspecified but large number of Sites of Special Scientific Importance, to be notified to planning authorities and owners; and for Local Nature Reserves to be managed by local authorities. For Scotland, the Scottish Wild Life Conservation Committee recommended (Cmd 7814) the establishment of 24 National Nature Reserves, 4 National Park Reserves, 22 Nature Conservation Areas and one Special Conservation Area. Both these sets of proposals were closely coordinated with those for series of National Parks in England and Wales, and in Scotland; and it was envisaged that there would be close cooperation in their implementation. One of the functions of the recommended Biological Service would be to manage National Nature Reserves, and to advise managers of other reserves, such as National Park authorities.

The translation of these ambitious ideas into practice not surprisingly involved a number of shortfalls in expectation, some clear at an early stage, but others only emerging after some years of experience. The first casualties appeared in the passing of legislation to enact the nature conservation programme. The National Parks and Access to the Countryside Act, 1949, enshrined the National Nature Reserve and the Site of Special Scientific Interest in law, but deleted all the other categories of area protection. It also set up the Nature Conservancy, with responsibility for conservation of physical as well as biological features, in place of the Biological Service. The idea of a series of National Parks for Scotland was dropped. Most of the National Parks proposed for England and Wales were established, but it later became clear that on the whole their authorities took much less account of nature conservation than had been hoped and, with the exception of the Peak Park especially, links with the Nature Conservancy were somewhat tenuous.

The Nature Conservancy proceeded with its National Nature Reserve acquisition programme, and at the time of its dissolution in 1973, had established 135 such Reserves. The Nature Conservancy Council has continued to acquire further N.N.Rs, and the total now stands at 150, covering about 120000 ha. A considerable amount of the N.C.C.'s effort goes into the wardening and other management of these. Additionally, there is in total a large number of other reserves set up by other bodies, notably, the R.S.P.B. and County Naturalists' Trusts, and many other areas effectively managed as reserves, e.g. National Trust properties. During the course of acquisition it became clear that there were many important sites which had escaped the attention of the original Wild Life Committee simply because of the inadequacy of survey knowledge at that time. Other sites again were found to have deteriorated seriously or even been entirely lost, so that alternatives had to be sought. This led to a need for periodic up-dating of the remaining list of sites for negotiation, but this was found to be an unsatisfactory procedure. In 1965 the Nature Conservancy therefore decided to launch a countrywide survey of natural and semi-natural habitats to identify as many as possible of the areas (including existing N.N.Rs) which could be deemed to have national importance, with a view to the eventual safeguarding of the whole series. This operation began a year later and involved not only survey teams of the Conservancy, but also much help from universities and the voluntary bodies. The definitive list of key sites was available to the Conservancy by 1970, but there have been delays in publication of the work, during which further new sites have been discovered and added, whilst others have been destroyed and deleted. It is hoped that the Nature Conservation Review will be published in book form early in 1977, as a joint venture of the Nature Conservancy Council and the Natural Environment Research Council.

This review is both an exposition of the range of variation in the plant communities and associated fauna of Great Britain, in relation to their habitats, and grouped according to the major ecological formations. This is intended as a background statement of what there is to conserve, and is followed by the identification and description of the key sites which are believed to be the most important in representing this variety. It attempts to provide a justification for the choice of sites by presenting a background rationale for the evaluation of nature conservation interest and the requirements for a national series. There is a definition of criteria for evaluation, expressing the range of interest and purpose placed upon the wild plants and animals of Britain, and thereby according measures of their importance. These criteria incorporate values mentioned previously, such as size of area and of population, diversity, degree of naturalness, rarity and fragility, which tend to identify the unusual; but there is also an attempt to ensure that the typical is adequately represented, especially when its survival is uncertain. They are applied for the most part subjectively, since the features being assessed are often not quantifiable in the present state of knowledge, and the evaluation process leaves a good deal to the judgement which goes with field experience. This may be open to theoretical objections, but the whole exercise has a pragmatic approach, in attempting to provide a firmer base for a site conservation strategy in the face of heavy and rapidly increasing pressure on the nature conservation interest of Britain. We cannot wait for the millennium in these matters. Key sites are being lost or seriously damaged at too high a rate.

The aim has essentially been to identify a range of sites which includes both the most outstanding and the most characteristic. But since the underlying intention is to defend the irreplaceable, in the belief that the replaceable is better able to look after itself, there is inevitably an emphasis on the special (according to the above criteria) rather than on the commonplace. The review identified 419 sites as being of the highest importance (grade 1) and 314 sites of slightly lesser or alternative but still national value (grade 2); covering respectively about 614 000 ha and 260 000 ha, and amounting to about 4 % of the surface of Great Britain. Within this total, about 70 % is uncultivated moorland and mountain, or intertidal coastland, and 92 % is land of the lowest or negligible agricultural value. There is within the total of 885 000 ha of land within grade 1 and 2 sites only a relatively small area on which future farming or forestry use is likely to be incompatible with management for nature conservation interest. A brief description of the main environmental and biological features of each grade 1 and 2 site is provided. The document is intended for nature conservationists, planners, landowners, administrators and others whose interests and activities impinge on land use, and it is intended also to be a source of factual information for biologists. The N.C.C. has notified all grade 1 and 2 sites as Sites of Special Scientific Interest and discussions are already in hand with a wide range of both official and unofficial bodies over the means of safeguarding the many key sites which do not already have some form of reserve status. Of the 733 grade 1 and 2 sites only 53 are wholly protected as N.N.Rs, and 450 have no reserve status at all.

The advisory approach

While the total area of semi-natural and natural habitat now set aside primarily for nature conservation is thus considerable, and to many people must inevitably remain the cornerstone of the whole movement, there has been growing concern to influence land-use policies in the country more generally, so that due account of wildlife and physical features is taken everywhere, not just in reserved areas. Moreover, there is in aggregate a large and important element of nature conservation interest, especially wildlife, which belongs to highly artificial and often fragmented habitats, which are not amenable to nature reserve treatment. To deal with this it is necessary to influence the thinking and actions of as many people as possible who have a direct or indirect influence on environmental use. This includes not only the owners and occupiers of land, but also the leaders of industry and commerce, the politicians and economists, the planners and developers, the exploiters of resources, the teaching institutions of all kinds, and the countryside-using public. In short, there are few interests or actual people whose activities do not in some way impinge on nature conservation, and it is necessary to stimulate an awareness of this relationship, in the hope of kindling or enhancing a sense of concern and responsibility.

This more pervasive approach to nature conservation has several facets. The bridge between the N.N.R. series and the advisory function is provided by the S.S.S.I. system. This covers sites of national and international importance (grades 1–2) and other areas (grades 3–4) which, although selected on a regional and local basis, fulfil an important function as part of the national series. Although these sites are notified to planning authorities and owners as being important to nature conservation, the N.C.C. has no control over their management, and can only express views or give advice. Nevertheless, the S.S.S.I. series, now numbering over 3500, has proved in practice to be an invaluable adjunct to the N.N.R. network through its corporate influence on the exercising of planning constraints. Many S.S.S.Is have been destroyed or seriously damaged, but it is likely that more have been saved or the damage mitigated.

This emphasizes the importance of good liaison with planners at various levels, and the N.C.C. is now putting a great deal of effort into this through Structure and Local Plans, not only by identifying important sites but also by advocating general policies and measures. In Scotland, an N.C.C. officer is seconded to work in the Planning Office of the Scottish Development Department. There is liaison with Departments at a variety of levels, and including both formal representation of N.C.C. staff on standing committees, and a range of *ad hoc* as well as informal contacts. Perhaps the best example of a field where the advisory rôle has made strong impact is through representation on the Advisory Committee on Pesticides and other Toxic Substances, and the Pesticides Safety Precautions Scheme. Here, the nature conservation view has been influential in ensuring the more careful use and control of pesticides harmful to wildlife, with the result that some of the worrying trends of the 1960s, such as the rapid decline of the peregrine falcon, have now become reversed. Liaison with the voluntary bodies for nature conservation helps to promote concerted views and action and to minimize unnecessary conflicts within the movement. As part of this advisory development, the N.C.C. is preparing a series of major policy statements on its views on nature conservation in relation to agriculture, forestry, water resources and minerals.

The task of nature conservation is considerably eased when the people concerned with the many problems have an awareness of, or, better, a sympathy for, whatever is at stake. Nature conservation as practised by a public body is seen largely as an activity directed towards the benefit of people. For many years, the official organization has thus put much effort into an educational programme, aimed at expanding knowledge of the resource itself, and the principles governing its proper use. This has been through talks and lectures, press, radio and t.v. coverage, exhibitions, and a variety of literature from N.N.R. and nature trail leaflets to parliamentary reports. Field guidance and instruction, both by wardens on Reserves and courses and seminars conducted by scientific staff have been practical contributions to the whole programme.

Legislation concerned with wildlife protection is an important tool, notably in promoting a favourable climate of opinion about the value of plants and animals as part of the natural heritage for all to cherish and enjoy; and thus in supporting other conservation approaches. It is important that laws relating to wildlife be kept under review, to cope with the changes in status of species, and to maintain awareness over problems of damage caused by certain animals. Both of these require periodic revisions of the law. The N.C.C. has been heavily involved in advising on the provisions of the recent Wild Creatures and Wild Plants Act, which gives protection to carefully chosen groups of rare and endangered species. New tax laws are likely to have powerful implications for the future ownership and management of land, including many areas of high nature conservation interest. The N.C.C. is giving advice on measures which would mitigate the effects of Capital Transfer Tax by reducing taxation for the owners of important sites who are prepared to manage these in the interests of nature conservation.

Finally, the connections with international nature conservation are wide and important, for this is particularly a field in which national or political boundaries are irrelevant. Britain has very direct links with the continental or even global conservation scene, for instance, in harbouring important fractions of the total European or World population of migratory birds, notably wildfowl and waders. International action with particular relevance to Britain includes the Convention on Wetlands of International Importance and the Convention on International Trade in Endangered Species of Wild Fauna and Flora. There are close links with I.U.C.N., U.N.E.S.C.O., the Council of Europe and the E.E.C. Environment Programme. The close collaboration with various international agencies has led to measures to harmonize legislation, promote conventions, set standards, safeguard sites and share skills in education and information.

THE RÔLE OF RESEARCH

Cmd 7122 placed great emphasis on the importance of research in nature conservation and envisaged this as one of the major functions of the official organization. The need for basic survey of the nature conservation resource was stressed, but there was also much concern for comprehensive ecological studies to further understanding of relationships and processes over the range of biota and associated environment in this country. This research was intended to serve the needs of

Reserve management in particular, and to support the advisory function in general, but was also seen as contributing to the advancement of knowledge, as one of the ultimate purposes of nature conservation. National Nature Reserves were envisaged as providing important study areas for research projects, with the advantage not only of outstanding scientific value, but also of unusually good practical facilities, including the conduct of research free from disturbance. Grant-aiding universities and other institutions in the conduct of related research projects was to be part of the total scientific effort and, where appropriate, research needed by the official organization could be done under contract by outside workers.

During the 27 years of their existence, the Nature Conservancy and Nature Conservancy Council have spent a large sum on research covering an extremely wide field, and its fruits are now part of the literature of science. The work has been spread over the major biotopes and a large number of species individually, and has varied from the simple and straightforward to the recondite and challenging. The results have, as in most organizations, been of variable quality and importance. Rather than attempt a review across the whole field of research activity during this period, I intend to draw upon a few examples of projects or programmes which illustrate different aspects of research required to answer practical problems, but which have also produced a substantial spin-off in the yield of fundamental scientific knowledge. Other speakers to follow will enlarge upon this topic and penetrate it more deeply.

Within the Nature Conservancy there was a rather early separation between work aimed at dealing with the practical problems of habitat management, and that intended to further understanding of the dynamic processes within ecosystems, as a strategic source of knowledge from which the answers to a range of future questions might be derived. The first was exemplified by the floristic surveys of chalk grasslands in southern England initiated by Dr A. S. Thomas, involving point quadrat analyses along line transects, on a range of important downland sites. These provided valuable base-lines for a monitoring programme when the unexpected myxomatosis epidemic of 1954–5 so drastically altered the grazing régime under which most of these grasslands had evolved. Coinciding in many instances with, or following, the removal of sheep through changing agricultural economics, the disappearance of rabbits led to profound changes in sward botanical composition which were measured by repeating the transects (Thomas 1960). The competitive balance between species was drastically altered, and vigorously invasive grasses such as *Brachypodium pinnatum* and *Bromus erectus*, previously kept in check by the heavy grazing, rapidly spread and swamped the smaller grasses and forbs which, in their rich variety, gave the former chalk grassland their high nature conservation value. Even more importantly there was typically a rapid invasion by woody species, notably hawthorn *Crataegus monogyna*, but also a variety of calcicolous shrubs, whose seedlings had previously been cropped down relentlessly by the vertebrate grazers. On the much more restricted chalk heath communities of some downs there was rapid invasion by gorse *Ulex europaeus* to form dense thickets. In either case the seral scrub replaced the herbaceous communities, through its competitive power.

From this there developed, especially under Dr E. Duffey and his combined botanist–zoologist–historical geographer team, a concerted approach to the management of chalk grasslands in order to maintain their richness in both vascular plants and invertebrates. Regional staff with chalk downland Reserves to manage also contributed to the general effort. The work included practical measures to restore or simulate the former grazing régime, by reintroducing sheep or by cutting treatments which involved the use of randomized and replicated experimental plots (Wells 1971). Scrub clearance and herbicide application were other direct methods used to reverse the succession towards woodland. The problems concerned with maintaining populations of rare and attractive but threatened plants, e.g. *Anemone pulsatilla* (Wells & Barling 1971) and *Spiranthes spiralis* (Wells 1967), were tackled by detailed autecological studies of the species concerned, and gave valuable information about the precise habitat requirements and competitive relationships of these. Attention also focused on the mineral nutrition of chalk grassland species, and the deleterious effects of both litter accumulation and fertilizer or manure addition pointed to the apparent dependence of the characteristic floristic richness of grassland on relative poverty of the soil in availability of major nutrients such as nitrogen and phosphorus (Green 1972). Studies of invertebrate populations in relation to specific food plant, height of vegetation and development of a litter gave information about the habitat needs of certain species and taxonomic groups, again in a way immediately applicable to management for defined objectives (Morris 1971). Finally, the investigation of historical documentation, in the form of maps and written records, has given valuable insight into the development of the vegetation and of the rôle of important factors, e.g. the part played by rabbits managed as a food resource, in the ecological story (Sheail 1971).

The commitment to management of woodland nature reserves pointed to a need for knowledge of the basic processes of the ecosystem, notably the germination, growth, reproduction, senescence, death and decomposition of the dominant tree species. This led to a desire for greater understanding of the balance between energy transfer and nutrient uptake and assimilation in the production of plant material, and the eventual breakdown of this by invertebrates and micro-organisms, with release of nutrients and their uptake into the soil complex again. Dr J. D. Ovington led a team investigation of this woodland cycle, which later became the foundation for a British contribution to studies of organic matter production in the International Biological Programme, aimed at studying the biological basis of productivity and human welfare.

These studies were conceived as an attempt to discover the potential capacity of different major World environments to grow utilizable living material, whether of primary (plant) or secondary (animal) producers. By measuring photosynthetic energy conversion and nutrient assimilation under different climatic, topographic, edaphic and management régimes and by different species and communities, it is possible to obtain some knowledge of the ultimate natural limits to organic production, and the deliberate manipulation which may allow these limits to be approached, for human benefit. The studies were chosen to include examples of ecosystems undisturbed by man, semi-natural types, and artificial crops, and it was felt desirable to study the performance of the same species under different environments, and to consider the different trophic levels within an ecosystem (Worthington 1975). In Britain, with its predominance of ecosystems profoundly modified by man, work began on production in three terrestrial types, semi-natural oakwood in Lakeland, moorland and blanket bog in the Pennines, hill sheep-walk in Snowdonia, and on one aquatic system, a eutrophic freshwater lake in the Central Lowlands of Scotland.

These I.B.P. projects required the use of experimental study areas which would be protected from interference and could be used for manipulative treatments. National Nature Reserves at Moor House, Snowdon, Cwm Idwal and Loch Leven largely satisfied these needs, but one special research site, Meathop Wood, was acquired for the purpose, since the experiments envisaged were unacceptably destructive on woodland Reserves selected primarily for high nature conservation value. The results of the various projects are in course of publication as a series of I.B.P. synthesis volumes.

Concern among landowners and shooting tenants about decline in stocks of the Red Grouse *Lagopus lagopus scoticus* and the need to manage grouse moors to the best advantage led to a team investigation of the population ecology of this northern game-bird by Dr D. Jenkins and Dr A. Watson. The work was based on the moorlands of northeast Scotland, and involved careful censuses of the study population at different times of the year, measurement of breeding success, and examination of relevant ecological factors, notably food, weather, predation, mortality through shooting, disease, and intraspecific behaviour. Preliminary findings were that the breeding population, which fluctuated in size from year to year, was determined primarily by the aggression of territory holders, which controlled the amount of dispersion between the end of one breeding season and the onset of the next, i.e. the size of the surplus populations. Low peck-order birds were displaced to marginal habitats, where their chances of survival were much reduced (Jenkins, Watson & Miller 1973).

There were strong indications that carrying capacity of the moorland, as determined especially by the state of the principal food item, ling heather *Calluna vulgaris*, was the ultimate factor determining numbers. It affected interaction between grouse, clutch and brood size, chick survival and adult mortality; and later work aimed to elucidate these relationships. There were clear spatial correlations between grouse numbers and fertility, in terms of base-status, of the underlying rocks and soils of different moors. Enhancement of the nutritional quality of *Calluna*, either by improved régimes of rotational moor burning to promote new growth, or by the addition of artificial fertilizers to the moor, had the effect of increasing breeding density, though varying time lags were involved (Miller, Watson & Jenkins 1970).

It was concluded that long-term population declines in grouse resulted from inadequate management of the moors concerned, and that an optimum burning régime, using small fires on a 10–12 year rotation, was the most economic way of improving grouse numbers (Jenkins, Watson & Miller 1970); the application of fertilizers over large areas is expensive. The finding that predators fed largely on a 'doomed surplus' of grouse which would die anyway lent support to the nature conservation view that birds of prey should be tolerated on grouse moors. The Red Grouse research has been developed further as a basic study because of its potential for reaching understanding of the mechanisms involved in the complex chain of causation which begins with carrying capacity of habitat and ends with regulation of numbers. Amount and quality of food determine nutritional state of the grouse, which in turn influences aggressiveness and hence territorialism, spacing and breeding density, but there is another effect on clutch and brood size, and chick survival (Watson & Moss 1970).

Anxiety about the adverse effects on wildlife of the increasing galaxy of synthetic organic insecticides, fungicides and herbicides led to the setting up in 1960 of a team under Dr N. W. Moore to investigate the problems in terrestrial, freshwater and marine habitats. Attention became directed especially towards the most serious of the discernible effects, on certain of the birds of prey, notably the Peregrine *Falco peregrinus*, Kestrel *F. tinnuculus*, Merlin *F. columbarius*, Sparrowhawk *Accipiter nisus* and Golden Eagle *Aquila chrysaetos*, whose populations and/or breeding success showed substantial and continuing decline in parts of the country where pesticide use was heavy (Moore 1965). Field studies of the status and breeding performance of some of these species, and others known to be exposed to contamination, notably the Heron *Ardea cinerea*, were complemented by the monitoring of tissue residues of persistent organochlorine compounds in samples of these and many other bird species found dead at random in the countryside. There was also supporting toxicological work with the same chemicals, but using mainly the small and prolific Bengalese finch *Lonchura striata* for practical and statistical reasons.

Rapid declines in breeding populations of peregrine and sparrowhawk were connected especially with contamination by the cyclodiene insecticides, the geographical and time patterns of decrease being closely correlated with both exposure to these chemicals and actual body loads of their residues. The experiments with captive birds confirmed the acute toxicity of this group of chemicals and suggested that the population crashes were caused by greatly enhanced mortality. These experiments also pointed to strong interspecific differences in sensitivity to the same chemical, a factor accounting for the lack of any significant decline in the population of the Heron, although this species carried the highest dieldrin levels found in any bird predator (Prestt & Ratcliffe 1972; Jefferies 1973).

Field studies had shown that low breeding success in several raptor species was connected with frequent egg-breaking by the adults, and the search for an explanation revealed that these and several other bird species had experienced a marked reduction in eggshell thickness. The onset of this unprecedented change was dated, by measurement of eggshells in private collections and museums, to 1946–7 in the Peregrine and Sparrowhawk, coinciding with the widespread appearance in the environment of the new insecticide DDT (Ratcliffe 1970). United States researchers soon found that many North American raptor species had shown similar degrees of eggshell thinning, beginning at the same time as in Britain (Anderson & Hickey 1972). These findings have led to a great deal of experimental and fundamental research on an international front, which has established that DDT is indeed a powerful agent of eggshell thinning, and which has led to a gradual understanding of the complex biochemical mechanisms, involving the avian endocrine system, concerned in this process (Cooke 1973). Current studies include electron microscopy to examine changes in fine eggshell structure, under DDT-induced thinning.

These four research programmes illustrate a number of different features. The chalk grassland programme is one which has produced practical results of direct importance to the management of reserves containing this habitat, and has made use in part of the facilities offered by certain N.N.Rs. The results have been made available in book form (Duffey *et al.* 1974) to all managers of chalk grassland and have been an important contribution to plant and animal ecology.

The I.B.P. work was conceived as part of an integrated international programme of fundamental ecological work which has nevertheless had human welfare as one of its ultimate concerns. It relied almost exclusively on the use of N.N.Rs as study areas, but was not intended to increase knowledge of how to manage these reserves for nature conservation. The value of the U.K. programme of production ecology has been mainly in the advancement of science.

The grouse work began as a response to grouse moor owner's concern to manage their ground and birds to the best economic advantage, and to maintain or increase shooting bags. The outcome is a good example of how ecological research can promote improved management of a wild species and its habitat, as a major national resource, while adding greatly to our knowledge of the population dynamics of animals as a major field of scientific interest. The work is not reserves-oriented in particular, and required the use of a special experimental reserve.

Finally, the pesticide–predatory bird research exemplified an approach to a pervasive countrywide problem – that of pollution – and shows how environmental management can be tackled on a broad geographical front through the advisory rôle, based on the fruits of research. The research itself is a good example of how simple observational field studies can provide a basis for detection of important biological changes and can lead to a whole pyramid of scientific investigation, ending at the most fundamental level.

AN APPRAISAL OF RESULTS

Looking back to the original hopes expressed in Cmd 7122, I feel that some have clearly been realized, but others have fallen short. The establishment of 150 N.N.Rs is in itself a creditable achievement, attained within the major constraint of the relatively very limited finance available for nature conservation as a whole. Some Reserves, e.g. Moor House and Rhum, have been greatly used for research, as the large numbers of published papers on both can demonstrate, but others have been under-used so far. They should, however, be seen as a long-term investment with a massive potential for future use in research, nature study, education and enjoyment of wildlife. In the context of planning control, the S.S.S.I. has proved to be a stronger tool for site conservation than originally seemed likely. The advisory rôle more broadly has had some noteworthy successes, notably in the field of toxic chemical and pollution control, and in helping to support the growth of the voluntary conservation movement.

Nature conservation has, however, not had the broadly pervasive impact on human affairs which the unified view of Cmd 7122 envisaged, through proper integration of differing demands on the natural environment. On the whole, agriculture, forestry, mineral and water exploitation, urban and industrial development and recreation do not go comfortably hand in hand with nature conservation for scientific and aesthetic purposes. On the contrary, they are often in head-on collision. This is not to deny that nature conservation should or could be a harmonious blend of various uses of natural resources. But this would require centralized control and planning in a truly integrated and comprehensive way, and this is what Great Britain conspicuously lacks. Planning is in the ascendant, but has virtually no control over the two forms of land use – agriculture and forestry – affecting the greatest part of this country. The use of minerals and water is also controlled by separate, autonomous bodies and only in part influenced by planning authorities.

The sectional character of these interests thus proves a major obstacle to any coordinated approach to land use, and attempts to do research or proffer advice which trespassed on the remit of other land-user organizations have tended to fall on stony ground. A central planning agency administering all land use seems a hopelessly unrealistic ideal, however splendid a concept it may be in theory. There is a *status quo* in the control of land use, and it is difficult to change this even slowly, let alone begin again from scratch, as would really be required. The result has been to restrict the rôle of the official organization to nature conservation in the narrower sense, and to increase rather than reduce the degree of conflict with other land users.

In Britain there has been general replacement of original and climax vegetation by derived sub-climax or plagioclimax types with consequent change in variety and abundance of associated plants and animals. This has resulted largely from farming and forestry developments over many centuries, but with considerable influence from hunting interests as well. Locally, more specialized resource exploitation has left a valuable legacy of wildlife interest, the most celebrated example being the Mediaeval peat digging which created the Norfolk Broads. Most of these changes involved the replacement of one set of habitats by another of comparable richness in species, e.g. in the change from woodland to mixed farmland with hedges, ponds, permanent grassland and arable. The tempo of change and the intensity of exploitation were such that habitat and species diversity were maintained over a long period, and some anthropogenic types acquired a high nature conservation interest, e.g. chalk grassland. Probably the biggest single loss up to 1940 occurred through the draining of the East Anglian Fenland, causing the extinction in Britain of a group of wetland plants and animals, and replacement of a once rich ecosystem by one of singularly low diversity.

The process of agricultural intensification has accelerated dramatically since 1940. Farmland which incidentally held a rich array of wildlife species in addition to the crops was subjected to now familiar techniques for maximizing crop production, which involve the relentless elimination of competing or extraneous species and therefore of most wildlife and non-productive farmland habitat. The capacity of the inorganic environment to sustain life is directed increasingly to production of crop species, at the expense of virtually all others, except beneficial soil organisms. Much the same principle applies to modern forestry, despite recognition of the amenity and recreational value of woodland. This clearly poses one of the great dilemmas for nature conservation. For at a time when the economic survival of this country demands that the land be made to produce as much food and timber as possible, conservation of the wild flora and fauna requires that the complete maximization of crop yield is not pursued on all farmland and forest. The problem is compounded for, in practice, this means asking some, rather than all, farmers and foresters to forgo some of their profit, since the money required for adequate compensation for loss is far greater than that available for nature conservation. Many farmers and foresters are extremely sympathetic to nature conservation, but they find increasing difficulty in giving real help.

On the whole, this problem is less acute over the conservation of grade 1 and 2 sites, on many of which existing land use is compatible with, or actually needed for, maintenance of wildlife interest; and it is greatest in the generality of the countryside covering the much larger part of Britain. Other forms of land use, particularly urban-industrial (including transport) development, and both mineral and water resource exploitation are also often in conflict with nature conservation, though the last two may provide compensations through creation of new habitats. These activities are, however, frequently a serious threat to grade 1 and 2 sites or S.S.S.Is. The use of land for defence purposes is often beneficial to nature conservation, usually through preventing other land use, such as agriculture, from intensifying. Use of land for game preservation has in the past been important in maintaining large areas of wildlife habitat, although the large-scale destruction of vertebrate predators is an adverse effect. The contraction of private wealth is likely to result in increasing break-up of large estates and intensification of agriculture and forestry within these areas. Recreational use of the countryside can often amount to over-disturbance for wildlife, and although recreation is part of nature conservation itself, it produces the dilemma that too many people will destroy the thing they cherish, so that regulation of their pressure is necessary.

Two general principles are emerging from the conflict between nature conservation and other land uses. The first is that nature conservation is increasingly expected to support its interest with hard cash, since its gain is so often someone else's financial loss; and the second is that the rationale and philosophy of nature conservation is required increasingly to be identified and justified as a valid form of public interest. It is appropriate, in the context of this meeting, to end by considering how scientists themselves regard nature conservation. I believe that viewpoints have tended to cluster into identifiable groupings. Among the scientists concerned primarily to advance fundamental knowledge in biology, geology and physiography, some accept the relevance of nature conservation in a relationship of mutual support, but others do not. Biological research at present tends to be preoccupied with fine levels of organization, and the aura of distinction has moved away from ecology and field studies. Many scientists see nature conservation as irrelevant to their interests and some are openly critical of what they regard as its hasty, slip-shod methods. A few clearly regard it as a misplaced use of funds which would be better spent on more important work. Another group is concerned with the application of science to the more pressing aspects of human welfare, and is often impatient with what seem to be trivial or even competing irrelevancies of a somewhat unrealistic and cranky nature. Yet another adheres strongly to the ideal, holistic view and seeks to integrate nature conservation in the narrow sense with the ecological approach to environmental use in the wider perspective. Beyond these, and including both scientists and non-scientists, are those concerned to defend wildlife and physical features for their scientific, aesthetic and recreational values, but including also people who believe that humanity has a responsibility to cherish the world of nature for its own sake.

I wish there could be greater understanding and hence cooperation between these groups, though there are limits to the reconciliation possible between the extreme, polarized attitudes. Some misunderstandings exist unnecessarily. There is a tendency to focus on what science can do for nature conservation, by way of providing a technology for achieving objectives with precision. But science cannot, in itself, improve on the objectives, because these are so dependent on value judgements. Nature conservation can do much for science by ensuring that the diversity of biotopes, species and physical features remains available for study. But it cannot make scientists study these things if they are not interested, or if they do not wish to make use of the special facilities, notably nature reserves, on offer. Nor is it possible to remove the elements of competition which arouse hostility in some quarters. The conflict with opposed land-use interests and their scientific supporters is inevitable and here one can only plead for greater understanding and toleration, including recognition that nature conservation has its own important part to play in human welfare, and that there is more to life than satisfying material needs or short-term economic problems.

REFERENCES (Ratcliffe)

Anderson, D. W. & Hickey, J. J. 1972 Eggshell changes in certain North American birds. *Proc. of the 15th Int. Ornithol. Cong.*, pp. 514–540. Leiden: E. J. Brill.

Anon. 1947 *Conservation of nature in England and Wales.* Cmd 7122. London: H.M.S.O.

Anon. 1947 *National Parks and the conservation of nature in Scotland.* Cmd 7235. Edinburgh: H.M.S.O.

Anon. 1949 *Nature Reserves in Scotland.* Cmd 7814. Edinburgh: H.M.S.O.

Cooke, A. S. 1973 Shell thinning in avian eggs by environmental pollutants. *Environ. Pollut.* **4**, 85–152.

Duffey, E., Morris, M. G., Sheail, J., Ward, L. K., Wells, D. A. & Wells, T. C. E. 1974 *Grassland ecology and wildlife management.* London: Chapman & Hall.

Green, B. H. 1972 The relevance of seral eutrophication and plant competition to the management of successional communities. *Biol. Cons.* **4**, 378–384.

Jefferies, D. J. 1973 The effects of organochlorine insecticides and their metabolites on breeding birds. *J. Reprod. Fert.*, Suppl. **19**, 337–352.

Jenkins, D., Watson, A. & Miller, G. R. 1963 Population studies on Red Grouse *Lagopus lagopus scoticus* (Lath.) in north east Scotland. *J. Anim. Ecol.* **32**, 317–376.

Jenkins, D., Watson, A. & Miller, G. R. 1970 Practical results of research for management of red grouse. *Biol. Cons.* **2**, 266–272.

Miller, G. R., Watson, A. & Jenkins, D. 1970 Responses of red grouse populations to experimental improvement of their food. *Animal populations in relation to their food resources* (ed. A. Watson), pp. 323–335. British Ecol. Soc. Symposium no. 10. Oxford and Edinburgh: Blackwell Scientific Publication.

Moore, N. W. 1965 Pesticides and birds – a review of the situation in Great Britain in 1965. *Bird Study* **12**, 222–252.

Morris, M. G. 1971 The management of grassland for the conservation of invertebrate animals. *The scientific management of animal and plant communities for conservation* (eds E. Duffey & A. S. Watt), pp. 527–552. 11th Symposium of the British Ecological Society, Norwich.

Nicholson, E. M. 1970 *The environmental revolution; a guide for the new masters of the World.* London: Hodder & Stoughton.

Prestt, I. & Ratcliffe, D. A. 1972 Effects of organochlorine insecticides on European bird-life. *Proc. of the 15th Int. Ornithol. Cong.*, pp. 486–513. Leiden: E. J. Brill.

Ratcliffe, D. A. 1970 Changes attributable to pesticides in egg breakage frequency and egg-shell thickness in some British birds. *J. appl. Ecol.* **7**, 67–115.

Sheail, J. 1971 *Rabbits and their history.* Newton Abbot: David & Charles.

Thomas, A. S. 1960 Changes in vegetation since the advent of myxomatosis. *J. Ecol.* **48**, 287–306.

Watson, A. & Moss, R. 1970 Spacing as affected by territorial behaviour, habitat and nutrition in red grouse. In *The use of space by animals and men* (ed. A. H. Esser). Indiana University Press.

Wells, T. C. E. 1967 Changes in a population of *Spiranthes spiralis* (L.) Chevall at Knocking Hoe National Nature Reserve, Bedfordshire, 1962–65. *J. Ecol.* **55**, 83–99.

Wells, T. C. E. 1971 A comparison of the effects of sheep grazing and mechanical cutting on the structure and botanical composition of chalk grassland. *The scientific management of animal and plant communities for conservation* (eds E. Duffey & A. S. Watt), pp. 497–515. 11th Symposium of the British Ecological Society, Norwich.

Wells, T. C. E. & Barling, D. M. 1971 *Pulsatilla vulgaris* Mill. Biological Flora of the British Isles. *J. Ecol.* **59**, 275–292.

Worthington, E. B. 1975 *The evolution of IBP.* Cambridge University Press.

Proc. R. Soc. Lond. B. **197**, 31–57 (1977)
Printed in Great Britain

Change in natural and managed ecosystems: detection, measurement and assessment

By J. M. Hellawell

*Directorate of Scientific Services, Severn–Trent Water Authority,
Sheldon, Birmingham*

Change is an intrinsic property of ecosystems. For effective conservation acceptable rates and directions of change need to be determined. A preliminary step is the development of methods for detecting, measuring and assessing the significance of ecological change.

Prolonged surveillance of 'natural' and artificially modified systems is necessary to distinguish those elements of change which are short-term fluctuations (cyclical or stochastic) and those which are part of long-term, perhaps irreversible, trends. Criteria for selecting appropriate parameters (for example, biocoenoses, community diversity, populations of indicator species or production estimates) are required, together with appropriate techniques for monitoring them.

Although few ecosystems are totally isolated from anthropogenic influence, those which remain largely unaffected serve as reference systems against which changes in intensively exploited or unmanaged (i.e. unprotected) ecosystems may be compared.

Introduction

The phrase 'nature conservation' is almost a contradiction in terms since change is an intrinsic feature of natural ecosystems. If we wish to conserve a system in its natural state we must ensure that the facility to change is also protected. In order to do this we must be able to detect changes and distinguish between those changes which occur as a result of the natural processes of the system and those which arise from external influences, especially human activity. When a particular ecosystem is rare or diminishing we may wish to preserve it and manage the system in such a way that further natural change is prevented. Such action necessitates the ability to detect undesirable change, knowledge of appropriate methods for halting or even reversing it, and means whereby the efficacy of the remedial action can be measured. Although nature conservation must involve many subjective decisions regarding what should be conserved and is not entirely unaffected by emotional, or even nostalgic, considerations it seems desirable that having determined acceptable kinds, rates and directions of change, the methods for detecting, measuring and assessing them should be objective.

[31]

INTRINSIC CHANGE

Intrinsic changes in ecosystems are broadly of three kinds: cyclical, successional and stochastic. In the short term, cyclical changes may be quite dramatic but often appear to contribute to long-term persistence of populations. Successional changes may be slower and give an impression of stability yet ultimately result in the disappearance of certain biota. Stochastic changes are, by definition, unpredictable but the resilience of many ecosystems enables a partial or complete recovery to the previously prevailing conditions.

Regular cyclical changes in population abundance are well known in some predator-prey systems, for example the lynx and snowshoe hare (MacLulich 1937) with a period of 9 or 10 years and lemmings with a period of about 3 or 4 years (Elton 1942). Among invertebrates the cyclical abundance of locusts has been known from antiquity and similar fluctuations have been observed in certain Lepidoptera. Many of these cycles have been attributed to climatic effects resulting from the sunspot activity cycle but there is, in fact, no correlation (Odum 1971) and such a mechanism would not explain the shorter cycles. Apparently regular cycles could arise from the combined effects of essentially random variations in biological or abiotic components of the system. Alternatively, they might be explained by inherent population–regulation mechanisms (Wynne-Edwards 1962; 1965) including behavioural 'stress' responses to population density.

Temporal successional changes may be inferred from studies of the spatial distribution of species or by direct observation over many years. Succession is evident in many plant communities where the growth of some species modifies the habitat and provides opportunities for the development of others. The process may be enhanced where the habitat is influenced by physical changes, such as the coastal deposition of sand, and is particularly clear in newly created or disturbed habitats. The characteristics of ecological succession have been reviewed by Odum (1969).

Stochastic changes are often observed following severe climatic conditions. The effects of severe winters on the survival of bird populations is well documented (Lack 1966) and also the influence of warm dry summers which appear to be conducive to the production of dominant year-classes in some fish populations through enhanced survival of fry (Le Cren 1955; Hellawell 1971). Floods and droughts are further examples of climatic extremes. Fires and epidemics of diseases or parasites may also be causes of stochastic change. The effects of some of these factors are often not only interesting but are known to be essential for the continued survival of some species, for example, in order to break the dormancy of seeds.

EXTERNAL INFLUENCES

The predominant external influence which affects ecosystems is human activity. The principal activities are urbanization and industrialization, with their attendant output of pollutants, and also changing agricultural and forestry practice and the increased use of pesticides. It is generally considered that these activities are detrimental to conservation interests, yet many habitats which we would wish to maintain, for example fenland drains, canals, coppiced woodland, hedgerows, chalk grassland and grouse moorland, are the product of human activity. Indeed, it is often the artificially managed habitats, with their subclimax environments, which support the richest floras and faunas.

One has to recognize that conservation of wild or 'pure' habitats and their ecosystems is relatively rare and most effort is directed towards the preservation of already managed systems. Thus we may conveniently define conservation as that environmental management technique which is intended to prevent or mitigate the direct or indirect effects of human activity upon ecosystems except where the activity tends to foster the maintenance of that system.

Conservation makes a valuable scientific contribution in preserving material for ecological investigation. A comparable situation to nature conservation may be observed in archaeology and especially industrial archaeology where the reasons for concern may be more immediately obvious: once destroyed or disturbed a site loses its scientific value and when important sites are discovered during re-development or construction, for example new town centres or motorways, prompt action must be taken to record or preserve them. Fortunately, the very activities which cause concern are also those which have highlighted the need, and sometimes provided the means and opportunity, for the discovery, recording and conservation of vanishing or endangered systems. The material prosperity created by post-war industrialization has also brought greater environmental awareness. The necessity for conservation of certain ecosystems for aesthetic reasons and in order to better understand fundamental ecological processes is now widely recognized. Without conservation the situation would be analogous to an experiment in which there were no controls and the various experimental conditions were unknowingly changed during the investigation.

SURVEILLANCE STRATEGIES

In the following sections attention is focused on the contribution of environmental surveillance, as a means of detecting, measuring and assessing change, to ecosystem management. The examples have been selected from the freshwater environment for two reasons; firstly, the greater familiarity of the author with this habitat, and secondly, surveillance in freshwater, especially in the context of water supply, pollution control and fisheries management, has had over half a century of development. Many of the techniques described and the conclusions reached are probably appropriate for other habitats.

The need for measurements

Some measure is necessary in order to detect and assess change, identify its nature (intrinsic or 'anthropogenic') and test the efficacy of conservation. It seems unlikely that a single measure would ever be adequate for every situation nor can one secure the alternative ideal of measuring everything. Furthermore, it is often only possible to decide retrospectively what ought to have been measured, yet any system of environmental surveillance must be adequate for future needs otherwise there is very little justification for its implementation.

The search for appropriate methods has advanced on two fronts; by selecting methods on theoretical grounds or empirically by field methods. The advent of electronic computing facilities has enabled considerable progress to be made in modelling ecosystems and investigating such questions as the extent to which ecosystem complexity and stability are correlated. It is interesting to note that the widely accepted view that complexity begets enhanced stability is not supported by theoretical studies and empirical evidence is not decisive (May 1973). It seems to the author that, although modelling can be of immense practical value in trying to understand ecosystems, the ease and speed with which results are obtained, the high level of sophistication and intellectual satisfaction associated with modelling have been detrimental to field studies. Good field ecology is tedious and expensive but it is essential in order to furnish the basic material for model building and to verify the theoretical conclusions.

Selection of appropriate measures

The ecosystem may conveniently be regarded as being built up from a series of sub-sets comprising individuals, species, biocoenoses, populations and communities, with each component contributing its properties to determine the character of the larger sets (figure 1). Surveillance may be undertaken at all organizational and trophic levels within an ecosystem, from the individual to communities, and each will contribute towards our understanding of the structure and function of the system. For example, the identities of species present can provide considerable information if their autecology and synecology are known. The proposition that many environmental insights would be derivable from consideration of a species list if tolerances, preferences and relationships of species were better known is attractive and has led to the concept of 'indicator' species. Criticism of this concept has probably arisen from disappointment with the, as yet unrealized, premature aspirations of its proponents. In reality, few species are understood well enough to permit their use as ecological 'litmus-paper' and the complexities of biological systems probably precludes such a simple approach. However, there appears to be no reason why, ultimately, all species should not be indicators, given sufficient knowledge of their ecology. Nature conservation provides adequate justification for appropriate research in this, otherwise unfashionable, area.

The individual as a unit, ignoring its identity, seems to be one of the least useful

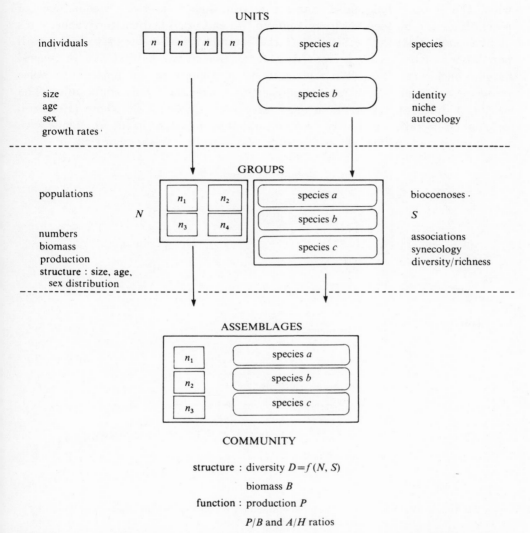

FIGURE 1. A conceptual framework of community organization and the structural or functional measures appropriate to each level. For explanation see text.

components for consideration, although it possesses physiological attributes which might be of interest. Groups of individuals, whether mixed or single species populations, are more useful and can effectively be used to detect spatial or temporal change. An interesting example of the use of populations without detailed identification is the use of algal cell counts or chlorophyll determinations to estimate algal biomass and hence potable water quality.

Biocoenoses or groups of species occurring together are qualitative attributes of ecosystems which are probably more informative than indicator species, especially when the normal biocoenosis–habitat relationship is known. Assemblages of populations and biocoenoses form communities and provide quantitative measures of biocoenotic attributes. Studies at the community level ought to include all populations of organisms present within the area of the habitat but, in general usage, consideration is often restricted to particular taxonomic groups since resources or expertise are rarely sufficient to tackle the whole community. The merits of different taxonomic groups have been reviewed elsewhere (Hellawell 1974) but a literature review showed considerable variations in the frequency with which groups are recommended for surveillance in freshwater (figure 2).

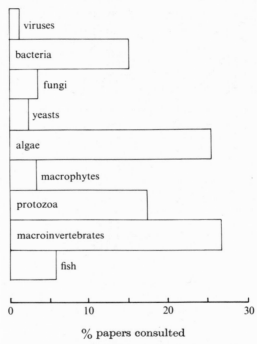

FIGURE 2. Distribution of taxa recommended for use in freshwater surveillance based on a literature survey.

At the community level one may measure the attributes of the components but there are properties of communities, such as diversity (the distribution of numbers or biomass between taxa) and production, which probably most nearly approach the ideal single measure mentioned above in that they integrate the many individual and group contributions.

LIMITATIONS AND CONSTRAINTS
Limitations imposed by selection

Although it is virtually self-evident that change can only be detected and measured in what is surveyed, Edwards, Hughes & Read (1975) have drawn attention to the danger of concentrating on restricted sections of the system. This applies particularly to measures, such as 'pollution indices', which are based on indicator-species. The situation is analogous to the signal and noise problem in electronic telecommunications: a high fidelity receiver with accurate fixed tuning will provide excellent reception on a given frequency but other signals will be missed. A less sophisticated broad band-width variable tuner may provide poorer reception and some intrusion of noise but this is compensated by the facility to scan a wider range of programmes.

The dependence of the detectable change upon the method selected is illustrated

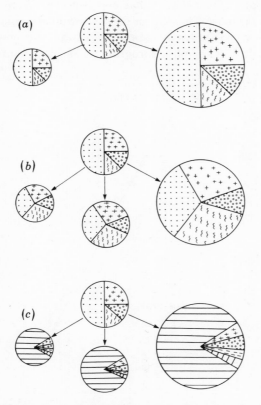

FIGURE 3. Diagrammatic representation of the possible changes in communities: (*a*) biomass changes, community structure remains the same; (*b*) species remain identical but community structure changes and biomass may change; (*c*) species and community structure change, biomass may change. Dynamic, functional changes may also occur, for example in production.

in figure 3 which is a diagram of the possible changes which a community may undergo, including changes in relative abundance or biomass of the component species, structure and total biomass. In situation (a) no change would be detected if surveys were confined to biocoenotic studies, but a simple estimate of abundance or biomass would adequately indicate change. Similarly in situation (b) qualitative analyses would be inadequate while in situation (c), although the species differ, the best measure of the change would nevertheless be a quantitative one. The diagram illustrates only the static structural condition. There may also be dynamic functional changes, for example in production or the autotrophic–heterotrophic balance, which should be substituted for biomass in the figure. Most changes are of types (b) and (c) although Hall, Cooper & Werner (1970) have described experiments in which nutrient enrichment increased zooplankton production without affecting community composition.

Constraints imposed by sampling

Even when an appropriate measure has been selected there may be difficulty in obtaining adequate samples. This aspect deserves considerable attention since it is evident that inherent weakness in sampling cannot be compensated by later data-manipulation. If the sampling programme is inadequate for the degree of

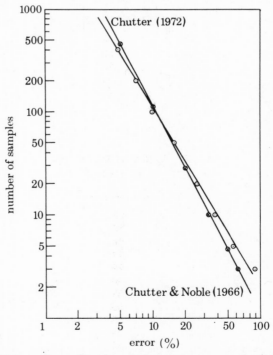

FIGURE 4. The number of samples of macroinvertebrates required for total population estimates with a given error and 95 % level of confidence based on data in Chutter (1972) and Chutter & Noble (1966).

sensitivity and reliability required then surveillance becomes futile. For practical purposes, the limits of detection are determined by the programme adopted.

Sampling difficulties are well illustrated by studies of freshwater lotic macro-invertebrates in the relatively uniform habitat afforded by riffles. Figure 4 shows the number of samples of macroinvertebrates which are required for estimates of the total population within a given error and at the 95 % level of confidence. The data of Chutter (1972) are based on recalculations of the classic work of Needham & Usinger (1956) in a Californian stream while the data of Chutter & Noble (1966) are derived from a stream in South Africa. That the two curves are similar is interesting but the important factor is the large number of samples which are required for reasonable accuracy. For example, it is apparently necessary to collect about 50 sample replicates in order to attain an estimate of population abundance within 20 %. The numbers of samples necessary for estimating the abundance of components of the macroinvertebrate fauna is sometimes considerably greater

TABLE 1. NUMBER OF SAMPLES NEEDED FOR ESTIMATES OF THE POPULATION DENSITY WITHIN A GIVEN ACCURACY AT A STATED RISK (Hales 1962)

		number of samples required			
		67 % confidence level		90 % confidence level	
risk ...		±5 %	±10 %	±25 %	±50 %
	accuracy ...				
site A	Ephemeroptera	2413	604	279	70
site B	Diptera	129	33	15	5
site C	Plecoptera	291	73	34	9
site A	whole fauna, winter	209	51	25	8
site A	whole fauna, summer	180	46	21	7
site B	whole fauna, spring	21	7	4	2
site B	whole fauna, summer	107	26	13	5

TABLE 2. NUMBER OF SAMPLES FOR ESTIMATION OF MEAN DENSITY (± 40 %) WITH 95 % CONFIDENCE LIMITS. R. CYNON (Edwards *et al.* 1975)

taxon	no. of samples	± % limits for 4 samples
Ecdyonurus dispar	27	102
Ephemerella ignita	15	77
Caenis rivulorum	26	102
Baetis scambus	17	80
Baetis rhodani	29	106
Leuctra fusca	66	162
Hygrobates fluviatilis	67	163
Ancylus fluviatilis	98	197
Potamopyrgus jenkinsi	84	183
Nais elinguis	24	98
Nais alpina	38	123
Chironomidae	10	62
total invertebrates	10	62

(table 1) and the number of samples required to collect at least one member of important taxa may be inordinately large. Recent studies by Edwards *et al.* (1975) have confirmed these findings for a British river (table 2) and shown that in any two random samples from the same riffle only 44 % of the species taken would be common to both.

REVIEW OF ANALYTICAL METHODS

Experienced biologists are able to make valuable assessments of the results of single surveys simply by inspecting a list of species and their relative or absolute abundances. When extensive surveys have been undertaken on an extended time scale for many stations as a basis for management policies at regional or national levels it is clearly impossible to use all the basic data. The problem is then how to reduce or condense the bulk of survey data and present it clearly and concisely (Beck 1955). A summary, usually an index, must be substituted and although some loss of information may be inevitable against this must be set an overall gain in comprehension. In many instances condensation or objective assessment by means of an index may provide new insights but numerical indices are, unfortunately, open to abuse, especially 'mathematical pseudo-exactness' (Elster 1966) in which essentially descriptive indices are given numerical values and then subjected to statistical analysis.

The selection of appropriate methods for the analysis of survey data has received considerable attention and recently reviewed by Southwood (1966), Clifford & Stephenson (1975) and Hellawell (1977, in press). Costs of sample collection and sorting are high compared with data analyses and the importance of making the fullest use of the results cannot be over-emphasized. Ideal methods are insensitive to sampling problems and taxonomic difficulties, easy to calculate, undemanding in comprehension, ecologically meaningful and effective.

The analysis of methods used in freshwater can conveniently be divided into three types: *pollution indices*, which have been developed from the observed responses of certain 'indicator' taxa to known pollutants; *diversity indices*, which describe the structure of the community and may be used to monitor changes in communities in response to environmental change; *comparative indices*, which may be used to assess spatial changes, by measuring the similarity of the community under investigation with others existing under known conditions or which serve as controls, or temporal changes such as those which might occur in a conventional 'before and after' study.

Pollution indices

Among the earliest attempts to provide descriptive indices of the stages of deterioration and recovery of communities in flowing water in response to organic enrichment was the 'saprobiensystem' of Kolkwitz & Marsson (1902, 1908, 1909) which has been modified, extended, and developed over the last half-century by many European workers including Liebmann (1951, 1962) and Sladecek (1965, 1966, 1967), and a most comprehensive review of these has been given by Sladecek

(1973*b*). Severe criticism of the saprobiensystem (Hynes 1960; Caspars & Schulz 1960) led to the development of other systems (Sladecek 1973*a*) which, although based on the concept of characteristic indicator species or communities associated with degrees or intensity of organic enrichment, were generally less formal (Warren 1971). Continental European developments in biological assessment of water quality, especially numerical or statistical methods, have been reviewed by Bick (1963) and Fjerdingstad (1964).

Almost all pollution indices have been derived from the observation of a progressive loss of components of a clean water biota with increasing pollution load. Kothé (1962) developed a simple index, the 'Artenfehlbetrag' or species deficit, which measures the percentage difference between the number of species occurring above and below a discharge but takes no cognisance of changes in relative abundances or the responses of individual species. Another index, proposed by Beck (1954), measures the difference between the numbers of 'tolerant' and 'intolerant' species, the distinction being made on subjective assessments of their limits of tolerance to organic pollution, but again no allowance is made for relative abundance. Other indices utilize the ratio between groups, for example King & Ball (1964) have suggested the ratio of wet weight of insects and tubificid worms but this seems both crude and naïve, as does the proposal of Goodnight & Whitley (1960) in which the proportion of tubificid worms to other macroinvertebrates is used. Brinkhurst (1966) considered that a useful index of organic enrichment was provided by noting the number of tubificid worms and the proportion of *Limnodrilus hoffmeisteri* to all other species. *L. hoffmeisteri* is known to increase in abundance with organic pollution but this index may vary with seasonal abundance. Indices based on the ratios of readily recognized taxa may prove useful in detecting subtle changes in water quality when one species increasingly replaces another where their environmental tolerances overlap. Examples are few but work by Hawkes & Davies (1971) has suggested that the ratio of *Gammarus* to *Asellus* may prove to be a useful indicator of organic enrichment.

In addition to the very simple indices described above there are several, more complex, methods for calculating pollution indices which tend to incorporate common factors, including an assessment of the relative abundance of each key species or group, their known pollution tolerance and their 'reliability' as indicators. There may also be a measure of the overall diversity of the community in computing the index or at least some recognition of the total number of species or higher taxa present. Only qualitative data are required in order to calculate the Trent biotic index (Woodiwiss 1964) but quantitative or semi-quantitative (relative abundance) data are necessary for the indices of Knöpp (1954), Pantle & Buck (1955), Dittmar (1955), Zelinka & Marvan (1961) and Chandler (1970).

The index may derive from the product of scores for each factor and in order to make the result less dependent upon sample size it may be related to the abundance of organisms by expressing the result as a quotient. The allocation of ratings for each factor is often highly subjective and the values used may be set quite arbitrarily. Identical index values may be derived from quite different combinations of factors: for example, a population of a few individuals of a sensitive pollution-intolerant species may gain the same score as that with many individuals of a ubiquitous, pollution-indifferent species. An index usually has a limited scale of possible values and may show reduced sensitivity at extreme or central values. It is therefore important to apply the indices to familiar circumstances or synthetic data in order to understand their behaviour.

Finally, in using a pollution index it is imperative to note that while the basis of the index may have ecological validity it does not follow that the observation of a given index value is attributable to the kinds or intensities of the pollution from which it was originally developed. For example, a low index, suggestive of organic enrichment, may arise from adverse physical factors such as low flow, elevated temperature or even toxic waste. Indiscriminate use of pollution indices may therefore, lead to erroneous conclusions.

Diversity indices

The use of indices of community diversity is based upon the concept that the structure of normal communities may be changed by perturbations of the environment and the degree of change in community structure may be used to assess the intensity of the environmental stress. No assumptions need be made regarding the nature of the stress which therefore obviates the inherent weakness of some pollution indices in that they are developed from the observed responses of biota to particular pollutants, almost invariably organic wastes.

It has long been recognized that in typical communities there are a few species which are abundant, several species which are less abundant and many species which are represented by a very few individuals. There is no general agreement, however, as to which of several proposed models is the most adequate description of this general observation (Pielou 1969). Examples include the logarithmic series model (Fisher, Corbett & Williams 1943), the log-normal distribution model (Preston 1948) and the ordered random-interval or 'broken-stick' models (see, for example, MacArthur 1957). Recently, May (1974) has shown that these models are all cases of the log-normal distribution. Their value in biological surveillance is that they provide a comparative basis for studies of stressed environments since it is possible to measure the degree of deviation from the expected species abundance distributions.

Simple indices which merely relate the total number of species and individuals, that is 'species richness', have been proposed by Margalef (1951) and Menhinick (1964). The distribution of the numbers of individuals per species is utilized in calculating the indices of Simpson (1949), McIntosh (1967) and in the information-theory diversity index (Shannon 1948; Wilhm & Dorris 1968). Pielou (1974) has shown that the Simpson and information-theory diversity indices are simply cases of the general function of a set of proportions (or probabilities) known as the 'entropy of order α' of the set.

The merits of these indices have been reviewed by Hairston (1959) and comparative tests have been made by Archibald (1972). Apart from problems associated with sample size, it may be difficult to interpret the results obtained from the application of diversity indices. For example, Archibald (1972) concluded that only high community diversity was related to water quality. Low diversity arising from severe physical conditions in the habitat under investigation may be observed even when water quality, judged by chemical criteria, is good.

Comparative indices

Temporal and spatial changes in water quality may be assessed from comparisons of two or more populations or community structures. The appropriate methods were largely developed by phytosociologists in order to distinguish plant communities in space or identify probable succession in time. These methods may be used in surveillance studies to identify spatial discontinuities between communities, which may be attributable to environmental change, or to detect and measure temporal changes between successive samples.

At the simplest level one may compare the species composition of the communities. Several indices are available but only those which compare joint presences (e.g. Jaccard 1912; Kulezynski 1928; Sørensen 1948; Mountford 1962) are preferred since joint absences may arise circumstantially and the close affinity indicated between samples or stations which had similar lists of 'missing' species would be spurious. Better comparisons are made with comparative indices in which the relative or absolute abundances of species are utilized, for example those of Czekanowski (1913) and Raabe (1952).

In using these indices one may compare successive pairs of stations or samples but comparisons of all samples or stations by means of a matrix are likely to prove more informative.

Another useful method for comparing communities is the 'distance measure' (Sokal 1961; Sokal & Sneath 1963) in which the abundances of species within the two communities are represented in an n-dimensional hyperspace and the spatial separation between these communities provides a measure of their affinity.

Finally, communities may be compared by means of ranking methods in which the relative importance of species in each community are ranked and then compared (Spearman 1913; Kendall 1962). This approach has the advantage that only the relative importance of species need be measured and sampling difficulties are thereby reduced. It is however possible to have identical rankings in communities with very dissimilar structures.

PERFORMANCE OF INDICES

It is not possible to provide assessments of the relative performances and suitabilities of all the indices mentioned above. Some basic properties of selected indices are given in table 3. Comparative tests of the performance of certain indice

TABLE 3. SUMMARY OF THE MAIN PROPERTIES OF SEVERAL INDICES

index	author	data† type	equation	range of values min.	range of values max.	comments
A. POLLUTION INDICES						
1. Species deficit	Kothé (1962)	ql	$I = \dfrac{S_u - S_d}{S_u} \times 100$	$\rightarrow -\infty$	100%	S_u, no. of species above outfall; S_d no. of species below outfall. Value of index limited by possibility that there may be more species below outfall than above
2. Modified species deficit	Hellawell (in press)	ql	$I = \dfrac{S_u - S_m}{S_u} \times 100$	0%	100%	S_m, no. of species missing at downstream site. Overcomes problem of unmodified index above
3. Relative purity	Knöpp (1954)	ql	$I = \dfrac{\Sigma(o+\beta)}{\Sigma(o+\beta+\alpha+p)}$	0	$\rightarrow 1.0$	uses no. of species in Saprobien classes; o, oligo-, β = beta-meso-, α, alpha-meso-; p, poly-saprobic
4. Saprobity index	Pantle & Buck (1955)	semi-qt	$I = \dfrac{\Sigma sh}{\Sigma h}$	1.0	4.0	s, degree of saprobity (Liebmann 1951, 1952; oligo = 1, poly = 4), h, abundance (1 = rare, 3 = frequent, 5 = abundant)
5. Saprobic index	Zelinka & Marvan (1961)	semi-qt	$I = \dfrac{\Sigma ahg}{\Sigma hg}$	0	10.0	a, saprobic valency in each of 5 saprobic classes (sum = 10), g, indicator value (1–5, 5 is high), h, abundance. Maximum score in each class gives quality
6. Trent biotic index	Woodiwiss (1964)	ql	derived from table provided	0	10	uses general responses of key macroinvertebrate groups: not taxonomic but convenient assemblages
7. Biotic score	Chandler (1970)	semi-qt	sum of scores derived from table provided	0	$\rightarrow \infty$	uses responses of macroinvert. groups and their relative abundance. Score in clean water rarely exceeds 2500–3000
8. Pollution index	Beck (1954)	ql	$I = 2C_1 - C_2$	0	$\rightarrow \infty$	C_1, no. of macroinvert. species intolerant and C_2, no. tolerant to modest organic pollution. Index rarely exceeds 10
B. DIVERSITY INDICES						
9. Williams α index	Fisher et al (1943)	qt	$S \simeq \alpha \ln N/\alpha$	$\rightarrow 0$	∞	S, no of species, N, no. of individuals, α, index of diversity. Derived from nomogram published by Fisher et al.

No. / Name	Author	†qt/ql	Formula	(low)	(high)	Description
12.	Simpson (1949)	qt	$I = \dfrac{\sum n_i(n_i-1)}{N(N-1)}$	0	1.0	n_i, no. of individuals in the *r*th... Higher the value, lower the diversity. Can be made comparable by subtracting from unity (Pielou, 1969). Alternative is to sum squares of proportions of species (Duffey 1968)
13. Information theory index	Shannon (1948)	qt	$I = -\sum_{r=1}^{s} pr \, \mathrm{lb} \, pr$	0	$\to\infty$	pr = proportion of individuals in *r*th species ($r = 1, 2, 3 \ldots S$)
14.	McIntosh (1967)	qt	$I = \sqrt{\left(\sum_{i=1}^{s} n_i^2\right)}$	1.0	$\to\infty$	n_i = no. of individuals in each species
15. Sequential comparison index (SCI)	Cairns *et al.* (1968)	qt	$I = R/N$	$\to 0$	$\to\infty$	R, no. of number of changes in species per scan. N, total number scanned. Can only be derived from examination of sample
C. Comparative indices						
16. Coefficient of similarity	Jaccard (1912)	ql	$I = \dfrac{c}{a+b-c}$	0	1.0	a, no. of species in community A. b, no. of species in community B. c, no. of species common to both
17. Coefficient of similarity	Kulezynski (1928)	ql	$I = \dfrac{c}{2}\left(\dfrac{1}{a}+\dfrac{1}{b}\right)$	0	1.0	as above
18. Quotient of similarity	Sørensen (1948)	ql	$I = \dfrac{2c}{(a+b)}$	0	1.0	as above
19. Index of similarity	Mountford (1962)	ql	(approximate) $I = \dfrac{2c}{2ab-(a+b)c}$	0	$\to\infty$	as above
20.	Raabe (1952)	qt	$I = \Sigma \min (a,b,c\ldots n)$	0	100%	a, b, etc. are minimum % values of each species common to both communities
21.	Czekanowski (1913)	qt	$I = \dfrac{2W}{A+B}$	0	1.0	W = sum of lesser measures of abundance of species common to both communities. A and B are sums of measures of abundance in communities A and B, respectively
22. Distance measure	Sokal (1961)	qt	$D_{jh} = \sum_{i=1}^{n} (pi_j - pi_h)^2$	0	∞	D_{jh} = distance between communities. pi_j = proportion of spp. i in community j; pi_h = proportion of spp. i in community h

† ql, qualitative; qt, quantitative.

have been made and will be published elsewhere (Hellawell, 1977 in press). In this section the results of some comparisions, based on two sets of data, one spatial, the other temporal, will be provided. The spatial data were taken from an intensive macroinvertebrate survey of a polluted river in south Wales (Learner, Williams. Harcup & Hughes 1971) and the temporal data were obtained from a nine-year study of an unpolluted upland river by Hynes (1970).

The general water quality of the River Cynon declined rapidly in the middle sections and this provided a useful test for the indices. The River Derwent had a

TABLE 4. SUMMARY OF MOST ABUNDANT TAXA OBSERVED IN A NINE-YEAR ANNUAL SURVEY OF THE RIVER DERWENT. RECALCULATED FROM DATA PROVIDED BY Hynes (1970)

Taxon	1955	1956	1957	1958	1959	1960	1961	1962	1963
Rhithrogena	743	494	512	415	203	160	2	2	3
Amphinemura	293	573	580	199	110	112	11	2	120
Isoperla	110	308	113	70	90	109	5	0	0
Esolus	254	54	107	16	357	165	482	351	133
Orthocladiinae	336	335	110	65	746	127	26	53	121
Hydropsyche	0	18	117	99	206	202	0	0	7
Baetis	168	115	1153	58	400	46	4448	1297	552

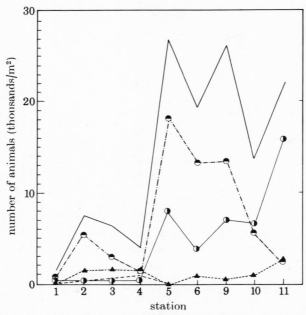

FIGURE 5. Total numbers of macroinvertebrates and numbers of major groups per m² for each station of the River Cynon. Drawn from data in Learner *et al.* (1971). —, total; ◑, Chironomidae; ◐, Oligochaeta; ▲, Plecoptera and Ephemeroptera; – – –, Plecoptera and Ephemeroptera, excluding *Baetis*.

remarkably stable fauna for a period of six years but in 1961 there was a loss of several important components and a dramatic rise in the abundance of certain species, notably *Baetis* (table 4). This change also forms a useful test for indices.

Examples of the results of using conventional biological parameters such as the total numbers of individuals, the numbers of taxa observed or the abundance of taxa are given in figures 5–6. These are quite instructive: the marked rise in faunal density in the River Cynon downstream of station 4, largely due to Oligochaeta and Chironomidae, and the loss of non-baetid Ephemeroptera clearly indicates the change in habitat through increased organic matter and suspended solids (figure 5).

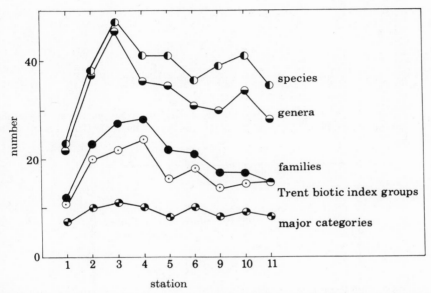

FIGURE 6. Numbers of five taxonomic levels of macroinvertebrates in the River Cynon. Trent biotic index groups are determined as indicated in Woodiwiss (1964) and represent convenient levels of identification. Major categories include: Coelenterata, Platyhelminthes, Oligochaeta, Hirudinea, Crustacea, Plecoptera, Ephemeroptera, Megaloptera, Trichoptera, Coleoptera, Chironomidae, Simuliidae, Arachnida and Mollusca. Drawn from data in Learner *et al.* (1971).

The number of taxa and artificial groupings such as the Trent biotic index groups varied with general changes in water quality (figure 6) but major categories proved too insensitive. The number of species was significantly correlated with the numbers of genera and families ($P < 0.001$ and $P < 0.02$, respectively). The paucity of species at the upper stations, where water quality was good, was attributed to severe physical conditions and low nutrient levels. In the Derwent the changes in the structure of the community are quite evident from considerations of total numbers of individuals and taxa (figure 7).

Index performance was assessed by comparing the direction and relative magnitude of changes with those obtained from detailed preliminary consideration of

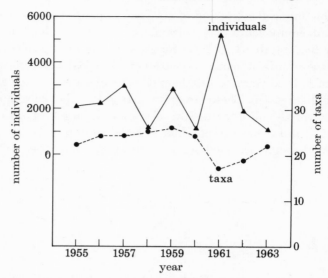

FIGURE 7. Numbers of macroinvertebrate individuals and taxa (species or species groups) taken in spring over nine consecutive years on the River Derwent. Drawn from data in Hynes (1970).

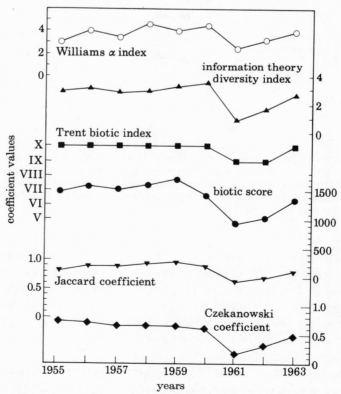

FIGURE 8. Selection of the results of the application of several indices to Hynes (1970) data from the River Derwent: Williams α index (Fisher *et al.* 1943), Shannon diversity index (Wilhm & Dorris 1968), Trent biotic index (Woodiwiss 1964), biotic score (Chandler 1970), Jaccard's coefficient (Jaccard 1912) and Czekanowski's coefficient (Czekanowski 1913).

the basic data and also in relation to the overall pattern which emerged when a subjective synthesis of all analyses was prepared. This strategy was considered to be quite valid since the main purpose in using indices is to provide a rapid summary of data which could only be otherwise obtained by lengthy subjective analysis. If, in addition, a consistent pattern emerged from the use of several different methods one might reasonably be suspicious of any technique which did not produce similar results, although it is, of course, possible that the consensus is unreliable or misleading. A few examples of results from the application of several indices are shown in figures 8 and 9.

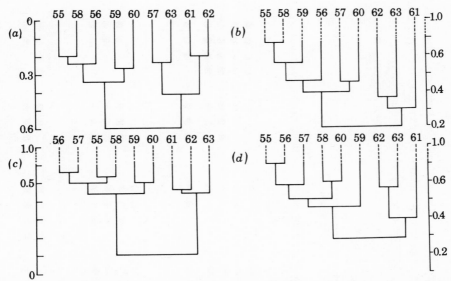

FIGURE 9. Dendrograms formed from Hynes (1970) data by average-linkage clustering using: (a) Sokal's distance measure (Sokal 1961); (b) Mountford's coefficient (Mountford 1962); (c) Kendall's tau correlation coefficient (Kendall 1962); (d) Czekanowski's coefficient (Czekanowski 1913).

Recommended indices for freshwater surveillance

A summary of the full series of tests is provided in table 5 where the expected performance of each index, its usefulness to management, the level of taxonomic ability required and ease of calculation are also given. From this table it will be seen that certain methods of data analysis appear to have more advantages than others. Of basic data, the abundance of given taxa would be the preferred method followed by numbers of species and total numbers of (unidentified) individuals. Since the numbers of genera and other higher taxa tend to be correlated (see above and Edwards *et al.* 1975) there would be relatively little loss of information if these were substituted for species. Among the pollution indices, including saprobic indices, the biotic score of Chandler (1970) is preferred when quantitative data are available, a view confirmed by Balloch, Davies & Jones (1976). Second choice

TABLE 5. SUMMARY OF RESULTS OF COMPARISONS OF EFFECTIVENESS, TAXONOMIC DEMANDS, AND EASE OF CALCULATION OF SEVERAL INDICES AND METHODS OF DATA TREATMENT BASED ON EXPERIENCE WITH DATA DERIVED FROM A SPATIAL SURVEY OF THE POLLUTED RIVER CYNON (Learner *et al.* 1971) AND A TEMPORAL SURVEY OF THE UNPOLLUTED RIVER DERWENT (HYNES 1970). NUMBER OF SYMBOLS INDICATES RATING, OPEN SYMBOL INDICATES VERY LOW RATING

index or method	expected effectiveness on theoretical grounds	usefulness for water management purposes	taxonomic demand	ease of calculation	subjective assessment of actual performance with test data	
					R. Cynon	R. Derwent
BASIC DATA						
total number of individuals	●●● / ●● / ●	●●● / ●●	○●●● / ●●	●●● / ●●● / ●●●	●●● / ●●● / ●● / ●	●●● / ●●● / ●● / ●
numbers of individuals in given taxa						
numbers of taxa (i) species	●●● / ●	●● / ●	●●● / ●	●●● / ●●	●● / ●	‖ ‖
(ii) higher taxa						‖ ○○
'species deficit' (Kothé 1962)						
SAPROBIEN SYSTEM						
relative purity (Knöpp 1954)	●●● / ●● / ●	●● / ● / ●	●●● / ●● / ●	●●● / ●●● / ●	‖ ‖ ‖	
saprobic index (Pantle & Buck 1955)						
saprobic index (Zelinka & Marvan 1966)						
POLLUTION INDICES						
Trent biotic index (Woodiwiss 1964)	●● / ●● / ●	●● / ●● / ●	●● / ●●	●● / ●●	●● / ●● / ●● / ●	●● / ●● / ●● / ●
biotic score (Chandler 1970)						

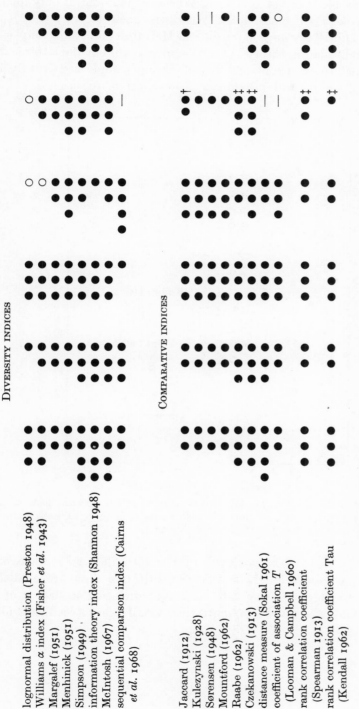

DIVERSITY INDICES

lognormal distribution (Preston 1948)
Williams α index (Fisher *et al.* 1943)
Margalef (1951)
Menhinick (1951)
Simpson (1949)
information theory index (Shannon 1948)
McIntosh (1967)
sequential comparison index (Cairns
    et al. 1968)

COMPARATIVE INDICES

Jaccard (1912)
Kulezynski (1928)
Sørensen (1948)
Mountford (1962)
Raabe (1962)
Czekanowski (1913)
distance measure (Sokal 1961)
coefficient of association *T*
    (Looman & Campbell 1960)
rank correlation coefficient
    (Spearman 1913)
rank correlation coefficient Tau
    (Kendall 1962)

† When used in full matrix, otherwise poor.   ‡ Even better in full matrix.

would be the saprobic index of Zelinka & Marvan (1966) and, if only qualitative data were available, Trent biotic index (Woodiwiss 1964).

The diversity indices of Simpson (1949) and McIntosh (1967) are simpler to calculate than the information theory index (Shannon 1948) but the latter is insensitive to taxonomic level (figure 10) and less affected by sample size than the indices based on ratios of species and individuals (Edwards *et al.* 1975).

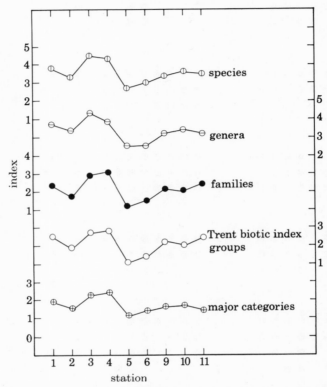

FIGURE 10. Information theory diversity index computed for species, genera, families, Trent biotic index groups and the major categories (as in figure 6) for each station of the River Cynon, based on data from Learner *et al.* (1971).

The comparative index of Czekanowski (1913) and the distance measure of Sokal (1961) are the most useful methods when quantitative data are available for comparisons. For semi-qualitative data the rank correlation coefficient of Spearman (1913) is probably best and for quantitative data Jaccard's coefficient (Jaccard 1912) is adequate.

THE CONTRIBUTION OF NATURE CONSERVATION

Conservation has an important part to play in the development of methods for detecting and measuring change but more so for assessment and interpretation. Since conservation areas are less affected by unwanted human activity, or at least are influenced by known management procedures, research into analytical methodology should be less confused by extraneous factors and may assist in the identification of those intrinsic factors which contribute to natural change Furthermore, conserved ecosystems may act as reference points against which changes in intensively managed or exploited systems may be assessed and facilitate identification of the degree of humanly induced change when the extent of natural change is known. This latter facility could prove extremely valuable since a weakness of the common 'before and after' study of effects of environmental management (for example river regulation, water transfers or impoundments) is that the 'before' condition may be unrepresentative, and an observed change might have occurred without any imposed environmental disturbance. Thus conservation helps to overcome common criticisms of baseline studies undertaken in order to generate 'impact statements' for management decisions.

Conservationists should guard against insularity: greater progress is likely to result from a combined study of conserved and exploited ecosystems, emulating the technique of physiologists, among others, who may learn more from the changes induced by interference such as removing parts or applying external influences than by observing the intact system. It is important that this approach should be encouraged since predictive ability, the acid test of any discipline, is poorly developed in ecology. Now that ecologists generally, and conservationists in particular, have aroused public environmental awareness and politicians, planners engineers and the like are concerned to take account of ecological considerations it would be tragic if we were at a loss to proffer useful, predictive advice. Thus, con servation has an important rôle to play in influencing general environmental policy and should not merely be confined to curating the few remaining relics of the pre-industrial society.

The author is indebted to Mr W. F. Lester, Director of Scientific Services, Severn–Trent Water Authority, for his permission to present this paper and for his encouragement. The views expressed are, however, those of the author and not necessarily those of the Severn–Trent Water Authority.

REFERENCES (Hellawell)

Archibald, R. E. M. 1972 Diversity in some South African diatom associations and its relation to water quality. *Wat. Res.* **6**, 1229–1238.

Balloch, D., Davies, C. E. & Jones, F. H. 1976 Biological assessment of water quality in three British rivers: the North Esk (Scotland), the Ivel (England) and the Taf (Wales). *Wat. Pollut. Control* **75**, 92–110.

Beck, W. M. 1954 Studies in stream pollution biology. I. A simplified ecological classification of organisms. *Q. J. Florida Acad. Sci.* **17**, 211–227.

Beck, W. M. 1955 Suggested method for reporting biotic data. *Sewage Indust. Wastes* **27**, 1193–1197.

Bick, H. 1963 A review of Central European methods for the biological estimation of water pollution levels. *Bull. Wld Hlth Org.* **29**, 401–413.

Brinkhurst, R. O. 1966 The Tubificidae (Oligochaeta) of polluted waters. *Verh. int. Verein. theor. angew. Limnol.* **16**, 854–859.

Cairns, J., Albaugh, D. W., Busey, F. & Chaney, M. D. 1968 The sequential comparison index – a simplified method for non-biologists to estimate relative differences in biological diversity in stream pollution studies. *J. Wat. Pollut. Control Fed.* **40**, 1607–1613.

Caspars, H. & Schulz, H. 1960 Studien zur Wertung der Saprobien system. Erfahrungen an einem Stadtkanal Hamburgs. *Int. Rev. ges. Hydrobiol.* **45**, 535–565.

Chandler, J. R. 1970 A biological approach to water quality management. *Wat. Pollut. Control Lond.* **69**, 415–422.

Chutter, F. M. 1972 An empirical biotic index of the quality of water in South African streams and rivers. *Wat. Res.* **6**, 19–30.

Chutter, F. M. & Noble, R. G. 1966 The reliability of a method of sampling stream invertebrates. *Arch. Hydrobiol.* **62**, 95–103.

Clifford, H. T. & Stephenson, W. 1975 *An introduction to numerical classification.* 229 pp. New York: Academic Press.

Czekanowski, J. 1913 *Zarys metod statystycznych.* Warsaw.

Dittmar, H. 1955 Die quantitative Analyse der Fliesswasser – Benthos. Anregungen zu ihrer methodischen Anwendung und ihre praktische Bedeutung. *Arch. Hydrobiol. Suppl.* **22**, 295–300.

Duffey, E. 1968 An ecological analysis of the spider fauna of sand dunes. *J. Anim. Ecol.* **37**, 641–674.

Edwards, R. W., Hughes, B. D. & Read, M. W. 1975 Biological survey in the detection and assessment of pollution. In *The ecology of resource degradation and renewal* (eds Chadwick & Goodman), 480 pp. *Symp. Brit. ecol. soc.* **15**, 139–156. Oxford: Blackwell Scientific Publications.

Elster, H. J. 1966 Über die limnologischen Grundlagen der biologischen Gewässer – Beurteilung in Mitteleuropa. *Verh. int. Verein. theor. angew. Limnol.* **16**, 759–785.

Elton, C. 1942 Voles, mice and lemmings: problems in population dynamics. London: Oxford University Press.

Fisher, R. A., Corbett, A. S. & Williams, C. B. 1943 The relation between the number of species and the number of individuals in a random sample of an animal population. *J. Anim. Ecol.* **12**, 42–58.

Fjerdingstad, E. 1964 Pollution of streams estimated by benthal phytomicro-organisms. I. A saprobic system based on communities of organisms and ecological factors. *Int. Rev. ges. Hydrobiol.* **49**, 63–131.

Goodnight, C. J. & Whitley, L. S. 1960 Oligochaetes as indicators of pollution. *Proc. Am. Waste Conf. Purdue Univ.* **15**, 139–142.

Hairston, N. G. 1959 Species abundance and community organisation. *Ecology* **40**, 404–416.

Hall, D. C., Cooper, W. E. & Werner, E. E. 1970 An experimental approach to the production dynamics and structure of freshwater animal communities. *Limnol. Oceanogr.* **15**, 839–928.

Hawkes, H. A. & Davies, L. J. 1971 Some effects of organic enrichment on benthic invertebrate communities in stream riffles. In *The scientific management of animal and plant communities for conservation* (eds Duffey & Watts). Oxford: Blackwell.

Hellawell, J. M. 1971 The autecology of the chub, *Squalius cephalus* (L.) of the River Lugg and the Afon Llynfi. I. Age determination, population structure and growth. *Freshwat. Biol.* **1**, 29–60.

Hellawell, J. M. 1974 Biological surveillance and water quality monitoring. European Inland Fisheries Advisory Commission, 8th session, May 1974 Aviemore, Scotland. EIFAC/74/III–1.

Hellawell, J. M. 1977 *Biological surveillance of rivers*. Medmenham and Stevenage: Water Research Centre. (In the press.)

Hynes, H. B. N. 1960 *The biology of polluted waters*. Liverpool University Press.

Hynes, H. B. N. 1970 *The ecology of running waters*. Liverpool University Press.

Jaccard, P. 1912 The distribution of the flora in the alpine zone. *New Phytol.* **11**, 37–50.

Kendall, M. G. 1962 *Rank correlation methods*. London: Griffin & Co. Ltd.

King, D. L. & Ball, R. C. 1964 A quantitative biological measure of stream pollution. *J. Wat. Pollut. Control Fed.* **36**, 650.

Knöpp, H. 1954 Ein neuer Weg zur Darstellung biologischer Vorfluteruntersuchungen, erläutert an einem Gütelangsschnitt des Mains. *Wasserwirtsch.* **45**, 9–15.

Kolkwitz, R. & Marsson, M. 1902 Grundsätze für die biologische Beurteilung des Wassers nach seiner Flora und Fauna. *Mitt. a.d. Kgl Prüfungsanst f. Wasserversorg. u. Abwasserbeseitigung zu Berlin* **1**, 33–72.

Kolkwitz, R. & Marsson, M. 1908 Oekologie der pflanzlichen Saprobien. *Ber. d. Deut. Bot. Gesell.* **26**, 505–519.

Kolkwitz, R. & Marsson, M. 1909 Oekologie der tierischen Saprobien. *Int. Rev. ges. Hydrobiol.* **2**, 126–152.

Kothé, P. 1962 Der 'Artenfehlbetrag', ein einfaches Gütekriterium und seine Anwendung bei biologischen Vorflutersuntersuchungen. *Dt. Gewässerkundl. Mitt* **6**, 60–65.

Kulezynski, S. 1928 Die Pflanzenassoziationen der Pieninen. *Bull. int. Acad. Pol. Sci. Lett.* B *Suppl.* **2**, 57–203.

Lack, D. L. 1966 *Population studies of birds*. Oxford: Clarendon Press.

Learner, M. A., Williams, R., Harcup, M. & Hughes, B. D. 1971 A survey of the macrofauna of the River Cynon, a polluted tributary of the River Taff (South Wales). *Freshwat. Biol.* **1**, 339–367.

Le Cren, E. D. 1955 Year to year variations in the year-class strength of *Perca fluviatilis*. *Ver. int. Verein. theor. angew. Limnol.* **12**, 187–192.

Liebmann, H. 1951, 1962 *Handbuch der Frischwasser und Abwasserbiologie* (two volumes). Munich: Verlag Oldenbourg.

Looman, J. & Campbell, J. B. 1960 Adaptation of Sorensen's K (1948) for estimating affinities in prairie vegetation. *Ecology* **41**, 409–416.

MacArthur, R. M. 1957 On the relative abundance of bird species. *Proc. Acad. Sci. U.S.A.* **43**, 193–195.

MacLulich, D. A. 1937 Fluctuations in the numbers of the varying hare (*Lepus americanus*). *Univ. Toronto Studies, Biol. Ser.* No. 43.

Margalef, R. 1951 Diversidad de especies en las comunidades naturales. *Publnes. Inst. Biol. apl., Barcelona* **6**, 59–72.

May, R. M. 1973 *Stability and complexity in model ecosystems*. Princeton University Press.

May, R. M. 1974 Introduction. In *Ecological stability* (*Workshop Papers*) (eds Usher & Williams). Chapman & Hall: London.

McIntosh, R. P. 1967 An index of diversity and the relation of certain concepts to diversity. *Ecology* **48**, 392–404.

Menhinick, E. F. 1964 A comparison of some species-individuals diversity indices applied to samples of field insects. *Ecology* **45**, 859–861.

Mountford, M. D. 1962 An index of similarity and its application to classificatory problems. In *Progress in soil zoology* (ed. P. W. Murphy). London: Butterworths.

Needham, P. R. & Usinger, R. L. 1956 Variability in the macrofauna of a single riffle in Prosser Creek, California, as indicated by the Surber sampler. *Hilgardia* **24**, 383–409.

Odum, E. P. 1969 The strategy of the ecosystem development. *Science, N.Y.* **164**, 262–270.

Odum, E. P. 1971 *Fundamentals of ecology*. Philadelphia: W. B. Saunders Co.

Pantle, R. & Buck, H. 1955 Die biologische Überwachung der Gewässer und die Darstellung der Ergebnisse. *Gas-u. Wasserfach* **96**, 604.

Pielou, E. C. 1969 *An introduction to mathematical ecology*. New York: Wiley-Interscience.

Pielou, E. C. 1974 *Population and community ecology, principals and methods*. New York: Gordon & Breach.

Preston, F. W. 1948 The commonness and rarity of species. *Ecology* **29**, 254–283.

Raabe, E. W. 1952 Über den 'Affinitätswert' in der Pflanzensoziologie. *Vegetatio, Haag* **4**, 53–68.

Shannon, C. E. 1948 A mathematical theory of communication. *Bell Systems Tech. J.* **27**, 379–423, 623–656.

Simpson, E. H. 1949 Measurement of diversity. *Nature, Lond.* **163**, 688.

Sladecek, V. 1965 The future of the saprobity system. *Hydrobiologia* **25**, 518–537.

Sladecek, V. 1966 Water quality system. *Verh. int. Verein. theor. angew. Limnol.* **16**, 809–816.

Sladecek, V. 1967 The ecological and physiological trends in the saprobiology. *Hydrobiologia* **30**, 513–526.

Sladecek, V. 1973a The reality of three British biotic indices. *Wat. Res.* **5**, 1135–1140.

Sladecek. V. 1973b System of water quality from the biological point of view. *Arch. Hydrobiol. (Ergebn. Limnol.)* **7**, 1–218.

Sokal, R. R. 1961 Distances as a measure of taxonomic similarity. *Syst. Zool.* **10**, 71–79.

Sokal, R. R. & Sneath, P. H. A. 1963 *Principles of numerical taxonomy.* San Francisco: Freeman.

Sørensen, T. 1948 A method of establishing groups of equal amplitude in plant sociology based on similarity of species content and its application to analyses of the vegetation on Danish commons. *Biol. Skr. (K. danske. vidensk. Selsk. N.S.)* **5**, 1–34.

Southwood, T. R. E. 1966 *Ecological methods, with particular reference to the study of insect populations.* London: Methuen.

Spearman, C. 1913 Correlations of sums and differences. *Br. J. Psychol.* **5**, 417–426.

Warren, C. E. 1971 Biology and water pollution control. Philadelphia: Saunders.

Wilhm, J. L. & Dorris, T. C. 1968 Biological parameters for water quality criteria. *Bioscience* **18**, 477–481.

Woodiwiss, F. S. 1964 The biological system of stream classification used by the Trent River Board. *Chem. & Ind.* **11**, 443–447.

Wynne-Edwards, V. C. 1962 Animal dispersion in relation to social behaviour. New York: Hafner.

Wynne-Edwards, V. C. 1965 Self-regulating systems in populations of animals. *Science, N.Y.* **147**, 1543–1548.

Zelinka, M. & Marvan, P. 1966 Bemerkung zu neuen Methoden der saprobiologischen Wasserbeurteilung. *Verh. int. Verein. theor. angew. Limnol.* **16**, 817–822.

Discussion

J. D. Holloway (*Tillinglea, Tillingbourne Park, Wotton, Dorking, Surrey RH5 6QL*). On a request from the Chair for comments on the value of investigations of ecological diversity to conservation methods and practice, Dr J. D. Holloway described some of the results arising from his five-year survey of the moth fauna of Norfolk Island, southwest Pacific, an extremely isolated island 34 km² in area. The survey had been quantitative, between seven and fourteen samples being made each month by local naturalists with a light-trap.

The total sample of about 100 000 individuals included all resident species (55) and enabled ecological communities to be recognized numerically. These were basically two: a small group of species restricted to the remnant of natural forest and a larger group recorded throughout the island. The size of the sample had enabled the complete species–abundance curves to be examined. They were found to approximate to the log-normal. Changes in the equitability component of diversity (measured here as the standard deviation of the log-normal) were then examined with regard to locality and season.

The survey period had included spells of extreme drought punctuated by months when rainfall was relatively normal. A correlation was discovered for the larger community of moth species between rainfall expressed as a percentage of monthly average and, with a three-month delay, the net population level of the moth community. The latter showed good linear correlation with equitability. Thus adverse conditions had appeared to produce, after a delay, a drop in overall population and an increase in equitability (the evenness of distribution of individuals among species, recorded as a decrease in standard deviation).

The general relation between habitat area, number of individuals and number of species within a taxonomic group suggests there may be a maximum value for equitability (relating to the way the individuals are distributed among the species in a community) which, if transgressed, will lead to a species number in excess of the holding capacity of the community habitat and therefore to extinction. In an unstable habitat like that of the widespread Norfolk Island moth community the species number will thus be determined by the equitability values attained during periods of extremely adverse conditions rather than by the mean value from samples taken over a long period of time.

Thus the study of the parameters of diversity may help to establish some of the constraints on the species-richness of a habitat and provide data that might enable predictions of the effects of area reduction or of potential tolerance to disturbance to be made in the development of environmental management policy.

Such predictions would be akin to (and may only attain the levels of confidence of) weather forecasts as they would depend for their accuracy on previous experience of diversity parameters over a wide range of ecological conditions. Observations similar to those from Norfolk are few and far between. They are needed particularly from extreme situations such as undisturbed tropical rainforest and disturbed temperate habitats where seasonal successions are more complex.

Proc. R. Soc. Lond. B. **197**, 59–68 (1977)

Printed in Great Britain

The scientific basis of practical conservation: aims and methods of conservation

By C. D. Pigott

Department of Biological Sciences, University of Lancaster

Most ecosystems in Britain, even though composed largely of native plants and animals, are to some extent subject to human influences and many are, or were, largely stabilized by agricultural and silvicultural treatments of long-standing which have become obsolete in this century. If the object of conservation is to maintain these ecosystems unchanged, then research must aim to identify the stabilizing factors, so that they can be continued. Experimental studies of vegetation form an essential part of this research. The changes in the vegetation of pastures on the mesozoic limestones of southern England following the cessation of grazing were largely predictable from experimental studies made before the first World War.

This, however, is to regard conservation as essentially concerned with maintaining a living museum and it is reasonable to ask why a particular state of an ecosystem should be preserved. An understanding of the factors which cause stability implies the ability to regulate change. This offers the possibility of creating ecosystems which are, for example, more favourable for the survival of particular species or more closely resembling natural ecosystems and therefore possibly more resilient and cheaper to maintain.

The British Isles contains a very great variety of ecosystems, using this term in the original sense of Tansley (1935), of which almost all are to a greater or lesser extent influenced by man. Since prehistoric time human exploitation has gradually increased and this has caused a continual process of adjustment in the structure and composition of these ecosystems. Yet even now, except for urban areas and land used intensively for agriculture, most ecosystems remain composed predominantly of native species. Surprisingly few species of plant seem to have been lost from the British flora and many have been unintentionally introduced and become established.

Overall the diversity of ecosystems has certainly increased as large areas which were once covered by relatively uniform forest have been replaced by a complicated pattern and wide variety of different types of pasture, meadow, heath, moorland, scrub and various modified types of woodland. However, during at least the twentieth century the rate of exploitation has accelerated and now diversity is decreasing in the lowlands, and often very rapidly within limited areas, largely because of the need and capability to increase productivity and profitability

Grasslands are heavily fertilized and reseeded, heathland is reclaimed, hedgerows are removed, scrub and woodlands of native species are cleared or converted to plantations. It is this change in the effect of exploitation from a long phase giving increased diversity to a new phase of rapidly decreasing diversity that requires an active, rather than passive, policy for conservation if we wish to retain many familiar types of vegetation and their associated animal populations.

Whether we wish or can afford to conserve some of these ecosystems is not simply a scientific problem, but, if we do, then the reasons for doing so have implications for practical conservation. If the chief purpose of conservation is to maintain an environment attractive to man, then the essential problem is to find relatively cheap and durable forms of verdure, both with and without trees. On the other hand, a scientific case can be made for wanting to preserve samples of the particular ecosystems characteristic of Britain (or any other region), simply to enable us to retain the opportunity to study and gain a deeper understanding of the nature of the world we live in. That implies preserving a particular array of species, and the practical problems are then of a quite different kind.

If it is accepted that there are good reasons for conservation of nature, then there is the problem of deciding what should be conserved. Again there are arguments other than those which are purely scientific, but the simple realities of what it is possible to conserve largely rest on scientific knowledge. One of the fundamental unifying concepts of ecology is that of succession and it is directly relevant to conservation. Few ecosystems are in a state of perfectly stable equilibrium, and most are changing or will change if particular restraints are removed. If the purpose of conservation is to preserve the existing state, then these restraints must be identified and retained. There is abundant evidence that human activities have been and are increasingly some of the most important factors influencing the distribution, structure and composition of existing ecosystems, even though these may be composed largely or entirely of native species. Attempts to conserve many ecosystems by removing human influence inevitably and predictably fail.

However, it follows that man can also harness his influence to serve the aims of conservation, but this requires analysis of what actually determines the characteristics of particular ecosystems. In order to identify which factors or their interactions are critical in maintaining the existing state of a system, experiments are required to discover what causes change.

There is no doubt that ecologists have been reluctant to make use of field experiments, even though their value was emphasized more than half a century ago by, for instance, E. P. Farrow (1917, p. 109), who wrote: 'it may justly be hoped that the employment of such experimental methods in ecology will contribute more materially to the sound advance of ecology than the laboratory determinations and deductive processes which are frequently solely employed'. Field experiments have the great advantage that the treatments which are imposed operate on an ecosystem as a whole and this allows interactions with the real conditions of the environment. However, for this very reason each field experiment is unique and generalizations depend on comparing experiments and also studying the actual mechanism by which treatments cause their effect. It is at this stage that experiments in carefully controlled environments have their true value. Much of what is regarded as experimental ecology is really comparative physiology and is often not shown to be relevant to field conditions.

A very real problem of field experiments is the long time vegetation requires to adjust to changed conditions. For example, changes apparently related to treatment are still continuing in the Park Grass plots at Rothamsted after well over a century (Brenchley 1969). For this reason, some natural or unintentional experiments are often very valuable in spite of the imperfections of their design. There is much which can be learnt by comparing vegetation on two sides of a fence, or studying the influence of zinc washed off the wire on the vegetation below.

Knowledge acquired from experiments constitutes much of the scientific basis for the technology of conservation, and it should provide the practical means both to preserve existing ecosystems, if this is required, or change them predictably to something more desirable. In fact, the wish to preserve existing ecosystems is often really to preserve those which have almost disappeared because it is all too often the process of disappearing which draws attention to an urgent need for conservation. One of the important activities of ecologists should be to develop methods for predicting the probable effects of changes in agricultural technology, rising costs of labour, tax-laws and such events as Britain joining the European Economic Community.

The recognition that ecosystems are disappearing is a measure of the rapidity of change because within a life-time there have been radical alterations in agricultural and silvicultural techniques. Many of the ecosystems which contain a large proportion of our native plants and animals are either the products of quite recently outdated agricultural and silvicultural systems, or are the modified remnants of more natural vegetation which have survived because of rugged topography, infertility, poor drainage or simply inaccessibility, but every year more of these obstacles to exploitation are overcome by increasingly powerful technology.

Many of the problems of conservation and the relevance of scientific study to their solution are well illustrated by the vegetation of the escarpments of the chalk and oolite of southern England. At the beginning of this century, the steep slopes of the escarpments were largely downland, the name given to pastures closely grazed by flocks of sheep and consisting of a very short turf composed predominantly of the following species:

Briza media	*Galium verum*
Festuca ovina	*Leontodon hispidus*
F. rubra	*Linum catharticum*
Helictotrichon pratense	*Lotus corniculatus*
Koeleria gracilis	*Pimpinella saxifraga*
	Plantago lanceolata

Carex flacca	*Poterium sanguisorba*
	Scabiosa columbaria
Asperula cynanchica	*Thymus praecox*
Cirsium acaule	*T. pulegioides*

The vegetation was remarkable for the large numbers of species, especially small dicotyledons, of which over 30 may occur within a square metre.

The importance of grazing by sheep and rabbits in maintaining the shortness of the turf and its diversity of small species was demonstrated experimentally with enclosures set up shortly before the first World War (Tansley & Adamson 1925). The result of stopping grazing was an increase in the height of the grasses and a gradual decrease in density, or disappearance, of the smaller species, apparently simply because they were shaded: quite soon seedlings of hawthorn and rose became established.

During the first World War, some areas of downland were ploughed, but there were also changes in the method of grazing and sheep were no longer kept in large flocks or were entirely withdrawn. The immediate effects were largely offset by rabbits. During the second World War, more areas of downland were ploughed, and then in 1954 rabbits almost disappeared following the spread of myxomatosis. At once, the changes demonstrated by Tansley & Adamson (1925) became almost universal and the smooth closely-cropped pasture rapidly disappeared. There was a general increase in the height of grasses but also a spread of tall species, including *Arrhenatherum elatius*, *Brachypodium pinnatum* and *Bromus erectus*. The immediate result was a decline and disappearance of many of the smaller plants, but it cannot be assumed that this would have been permanent. It has been shown by Watt (1957) on similar grassland over chalky-drift in Breckland that this initial phase of dominance by grasses gradually gives way to a more uneven sward in which the vigour of grasses declines patchily and dicotyledons reappear. This change is also seen following the spread of *Brachypodium pinnatum*. Once established this rhizomatous grass spreads vegetatively to form dense circular patches, but as these grow larger exclusive dominance is maintained only in an outer zone, where of the original vegetation only *Poterium sanguisorba* and some *Festuca ovina* persist. Towards the centre vigour decreases, the shoots become scattered, flowering almost ceases and many of the smaller species reappear. A much more fundamental change in the vegetation is caused by the spread of hawthorn and other shrubs because it leads eventually to elimination of almost all the species of open grasslands.

Possibly as a result of seeing that a tall grassland or scrub could develop even on the steep slopes, attempts were made to reseed downland. Although attempts to grow cereals on the shallowest soils had frequently failed, it was found that application of nitrogen, phosphorus and potassium to downland allowed establishment of more productive grasses such as rye-grass and timothy with the complete disappearance of the original species. In fact, it is clear that the original vegetation dominated by *Festuca ovina* exists within a very narrow range of chemical conditions. Areas of downland ploughed during the two world wars and then abandoned are not recolonized by *Festuca ovina* for many decades, but are characterized by a patchy vegetation of stunted shrubs, often *Cornus sanguinea*, and mainly dicotyledons (Lloyd & Pigott 1967). Small additions of inorganic nitrogen, or of phosphate if members of the Leguminosae are present, allow the development of a typical downland turf of *Festuca ovina* and *F. rubra* (table 1), but larger applications allow these species to be replaced by those which are more productive. A similar change can result from large numbers of people using downland for recreation.

TABLE 1. DRY MASS OF SHOOTS OF *FESTUCA OVINA* IN JULY 1964 FOLLOWING ADDITIONS OF NITROGEN AND PHOSPHORUS TO SPARSE VEGETATION ON CHALK IN 1963 (g/m^2) (from Lloyd & Pigott 1967)

−	+P	+N	+PN
35	55	146	197

Quite clearly downland of the type described by Tansley & Adamson (1926) cannot be preserved simply by preventing ploughing or reseeding. Either grazing must be maintained, or an attempt made to imitate the effects of grazing by mowing. It is also clear that downland is largely, if not entirely, the product of a particular agricultural practice, so it may well be asked why we should wish to preserve what is plainly an artificial ecosystem. There are a number of reasons: it is an ecosystem which is very rich in species, both plants and animals (particularly insects), many of which are characteristic of central and southern Europe and at their northern limit in England. Some of these species, for example *Carex humilis*, *Herminium monorchis*, *Ophrys fuciflora*, *O. aranifera*, *Anemone pulsatilla*, *Bunium bulbocastanum*, *Phyteuma tenerum*, *Polygala calcarea*, *Senecio integrifolius* and *Thesium humifusum* are now virtually confined to this type of grassland on chalk and oolite, so that with the loss of downland they are likely to become very rare or extinct.

Those concerned with conservation are often criticized for being obsessed with rare species but it is, of course, these organisms which are most at risk and which, in fact, give many ecosystems their particular character. It should be emphasized that there are important differences between types of rare species, some of which are casual weeds whose appearance is often temporary and largely fortuitous. In contrast, all the species mentioned seem to be critically dependent for their survival on the particular conditions of downland turf and, far from being fortuitous in their occurrence, they are very exacting. They may be thought of as the aristocratic species of downland because they are often restricted to those areas of grassland which have been least disturbed and have probably remained unploughed since early historic or even prehistoric times. Conservation of such species depends either on retaining their habitat unchanged, or discovering the cause of their apparent immobility.

Aster linosyris provides an interesting example of this type of plant, although it does not occur on mesozoic limestones in England. It is a southern-continental species which occurs on chalk and limestone in France but is restricted to south-facing cliffs of Devonian or Carboniferous limestone on the west coast of Britain. It flowers in late summer and no fertile fruits (achenes) have been obtained from its northernmost localities. Cuttings of plants from several populations were grown in Sheffield and a small proportion of achenes were fertile. The proportion can be altered by the simple experiment of dividing the flowering shoots of single plants with small screens of asbestos, so that flower-heads, but not the leaves, are either fully exposed to sun or shaded. In 1969 the average number of achenes containing embryos in each flower-head was 14.1 on the south side and 0.57 on the north: a difference which is significant at $P = 0.001$. The temperature of the flowers on the two sides differs by about 5 °C on a sunny afternoon.

It might seem that failure to set fertile achenes in the British localities is therefore simply determined by climate. However, the temperature of flower-heads was also raised a similar amount by enclosing flowers in transparent bags which behave like small glass-houses (Geiger 1965). Surprisingly no embryos developed and further study shows the populations from northwest England are self-incompatible. Moreover, a small population on Humphrey Head in Lancashire consists of a single self-incompatible clone and so also are all the populations on the Great Orme which have been tested, but when grown with plants from other populations at Lancaster, all produce fertile achenes and are often surrounded by seedlings. Self-incompatibility is itself influenced by temperatures (Lewis 1942) and isolated plants of *A. linosyris* grown against a south-facing wall in Cambridge can produce a very low proportion of fertile achenes. This is possibly an extreme example, but it demonstrates how precarious is the survival of such 'populations' and how vulnerable they are likely to be to changes in their environment.

The problems of conserving not only downland, but all lowland grasslands, is the rapidity with which they are invaded by woodland when grazing is relaxed. This is shown convincingly by Geescroft Wilderness at Rothamsted where now quite dense woodland of oak (*Quercus robur*) and ash (*Fraxinus excelsior*) occupies land which was rough grassland at the end of the nineteenth century and carried arable crops in 1885. These trees established themselves naturally and the hawthorns which gave the first oaks protection are still present, but some are dying. Early stages of this process can be seen nearby on Harpenden Common. When compared with woodlands in the same region which are known to be of considerable antiquity, several obvious differences emerge. In Geescroft the structure is high-forest with the trees irregularly scattered and some in groups; there is an understorey of holly and thickets of elm (*Ulmus procera*). Old woodlands, in contrast, have evenly-spaced large oaks with an understorey of many-stemmed bushes of hazel (*Corylus avellana*) and hornbeam (*Carpinus betulus*). This structure of coppice-with-standards is the product of an ancient silvicultural system, which has only died out in this century, and to this extent the structure of the woodland is quite artificial. Coppice-with-standards is, or was until recently, characteristic of almost all ancient woodlands in the lowlands, and there is often documentary evidence that the actual woodlands occupied more or less the same sites in the Middle Ages and may, in fact, have been derived from woodlands of the manorial wastes. This is why they often are situated at the boundaries of parishes. Paradoxically then, woodlands which have the strongest claim to be regarded as ancient, usually have the least natural structure.

Comparison of recent and ancient woodlands shows another striking difference. All old woodlands near Rothamsted contain the familiar species of English woodlands, such as *Mercurialis perennis, Endymion non-scriptus, Primula vulgaris, Anemone nemoralis, Oxalis acetosella, Milium effusum* and some less common species, for example, *Narcissus pseudo-narcissus*. A survey in 1974 showed that most of these species are conspicuously absent from Geescroft Wilderness and the present distribution of *Mercurialis perennis* (figure 1) and *Endymion non-scriptus*

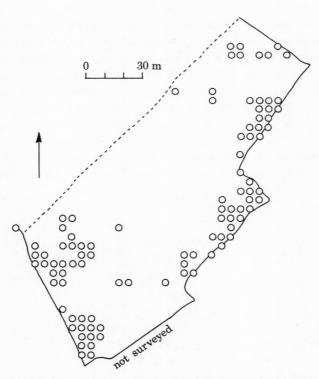

FIGURE 1. Distribution of *Mercurialis perennis* in Geescroft Wilderness, Rothamsted, Hertfordshire, based on a survey in 1973–4. Solid lines are old hedgerows and the broken line a fence separating the Wilderness from the adjacent field. The southeast extremity is influenced by the adjacent road and was not surveyed.

shows clearly that they have been derived from the old boundary hedges and to judge from recent woodlands elsewhere might otherwise be absent altogether.

In fact, a very large proportion of true woodland plants, including such common species as *Anemone nemorosa* and many less common species both woody (e.g. *Crataegus laevigata, Sorbus torminalis, Tilia cordata*) and herbaceous (e.g. *Carex strigosa, Convallaria majalis, Primula elatior, Polygonatum multiflorum*) are restricted almost entirely to ancient woodlands or sometimes old hedgerows, and are absent from recent woodlands, whether or not they were planted. For the sake of their rich assemblage of woodland species, it is the ancient woodlands with their largely artificial structure which tend to be selected for conservation with all the attendant difficulties of trying to maintain the artificial structure. Coppicing, the regular cutting of the underwood, was generally abandoned between 1914 and 1939 with a final episode in many woods in 1947. During the first World War the standards were extracted from many woods and not replaced. Now after up to half a century of neglect the understorey has grown up and casts a deep shade, so that only the most shade-tolerant herbaceous species are abundant and most other species are suppressed. Woodlands in the Weald which when still coppiced in about 1935 had a herbaceous layer composed of *Primula vulgaris, Anemone nemorosa* and *Endymion non-scriptus* in great abundance with sparse *Mercurialis perennis*, now are dominated almost exclusively by the latter species. Two experiments show why this has happened. *Mercurialis* produces a new crop of shoots in early spring which last through the whole summer. If they are cut off they are not replaced in the same year, so that it is a simple matter to reduce the density of shoots. When this is done surviving plants of *Endymion* and *Primula* begin to flower and reproduce freely from seed; in a few years they replace *Mercurialis* (table 2). It may also be shown

TABLE 2. EFFECT OF REMOVAL OF SHOOTS OF *MERCURIALIS PERENNIS* IN PLOTS IN BUFF WOOD, CAMBRIDGESHIRE. Figures are estimated cover

	shoots removed		undisturbed	
	1961	1964	1961	1964
Mercurialis perennis	95	0	95	95
Endymion non-scriptus	20	60	20	20
Primula vulgaris	1	15	1	1
Poa trivialis	+	30	+	1
Glechoma hederacea	1	10	1	5
Ranunculus ficaria	1	5	1	1
Fraxinus excelsior (seedlings)	+	1	+	−
Viola riviniana	1	1	−	−
Cornus sanguinea (seedling)	+	1	−	−
Mnium undulatum	+	5	+	+
Geum urbanum	−	5	−	−
Fragaria vesca	−	1	−	−
Arctium vulgare	−	1	−	−
inflorescences of *Endymion non-scriptus* per m²	5	17	7	1

by simple experiments that *Mercurialis* is very sensitive to even occasional trampling and with this treatment its density declines (table 3). Its failure to achieve exclusive dominance with the frequent disturbance of coppicing is easily explained.

TABLE 3. MEAN AND 95% CONFIDENCE LIMITS OF NUMBERS OF SHOOTS OF *MERCURIALIS PERENNIS* IN $0.5 \text{ m} \times 0.5 \text{ m}$ PLOTS, UNDAMAGED OR OCCASIONALLY TRAMPLED; THRANG WOOD, LANCASHIRE 1971–2

undamaged	71	± 9.1
trampled	29	± 8.6

Although woodlands change more slowly than grasslands, they change nevertheless and action is needed if the aim of conservation is to retain the original structure. There are compelling reasons for wanting to do this. Quite apart from preserving the varied and incidentally very beautiful woodland flora, it has been shown by Rackham (1976) that ancient woodlands contain a great store of historical features, including ancient boundary banks separating parcels with different histories of silvicultural treatment often reflected in the nature of the soils and distribution of plants. There is a rich harvest of ecological knowledge yet to be gathered from what may be regarded as very long-established experiments.

There is, however, another possible course of action for conserving woodlands and one which has much to commend it in terms of increasing scientific knowledge of the natural world. There are still fragments of deciduous forest in Europe, which are not known to have ever been subjected to any silvicultural treatment and retain many of the features of virgin forest. Perhaps the most famous is the great forest of Białowieża in eastern Poland. Such woodland is self-perpetuating and also contains an extraordinarily varied assemblage of woodland species. Woodlands may thus display on a large scale the features demonstrated by Watt (1957) for grasslands. The uniformity of neglected coppice is probably transitory and once a complex uneven-aged structure develops, then a more varied assemblage of woodland species might be restored.

We certainly have enough knowledge obtained from pollen-analysis and ecological studies to predict the composition of the tree-canopy of natural forest in the English lowlands. What conditions control regeneration and where the herbaceous species fit into the structure would have yet to be discovered experimentally and it might well prove necessary to reintroduce some of our extinct woodland fauna, in particular, wild boar. To attempt to reconstruct some areas of more natural forest in Britain would be an ecological experiment on a grand scale, but a venture which might help to restore the confidence of future generations in the wisdom of their twentieth-century ancestors.

REFERENCES (Pigott)

Brenchley, W. W. (revised by Warington, K.) 1969 *The Park Grass plots at Rothamsted 1856-1949*. Harpenden: Rothamsted Experimental Station.

Farrow, E. P. 1917 On the ecology of the vegetation of Breckland. 4. Experiments mainly relating to the available water supply *J. Ecol.* **5**, 104–113.

Geiger, R. 1965 *The climate near the ground*. Cambridge, Massachusetts: Harvard University Press.

Lewis, D. 1942 The physiology of incompatibility: 1. The effect of temperature. *Proc. R. Soc. Lond.* B **131**, 13.

Lloyd, P. S. & Pigott, C. D. 1967 The influence of soil conditions on the course of succession on the chalk of southern England. *J. Ecol.* **55**, 137–146.

Rackham, O. 1976 *Trees and woodland in the British landscape*. London: Dent.

Tansley, A. G. & Adamson, R. S. 1925 Studies of the vegetation of the English chalk: 3. The chalk grasslands of the Hampshire–Sussex border. *J. Ecol.* **13**, 177–223.

Tansley, A. G. & Adamson, R. S. 1926 A preliminary survey of the chalk grasslands of the Sussex Downs. *J. Ecol.* **14**, 1–32.

Tansley, A. G. 1935 The use and abuse of vegetational concepts and terms. *Ecology* **16**, 284–307.

Watt, A. S. 1957 The effect of excluding rabbits from grassland B (Mesobrometum) in Breckland. *J. Ecol.* **45**, 861–878.

S. M. WALTERS (*University Botanic Garden, Cambridge*). Following the Chairman's remarks on Professor Pigott's excellent paper, may I make a plea that we should look at conservation problems on a *world scale*? (I realize that the title of this meeting would make much discussion of world conservation problems inappropriate, but feel that some mention of the world dimension is essential). As President of a County Naturalists' Trust, I am, of course, aware of the value of local conservation, but I hope that this would be in the wider context of national conservation – which itself ought to be set in the widest possible context of the whole world. Much of our thinking at present stops at the *national* level. Should not our National Nature Reserves, for example, be assessed on a world scale?

Proc. R. Soc. Lond. B. **197**, 69–76 (1977)

Printed in Great Britain

The scientific basis of practical conservation: factors limiting the persistence of populations and communities of animals and plants

By J. P. DEMPSTER

Institute of Terrestrial Ecology, Monks Wood Experimental Station, Abbots Ripton, Huntingdon, Cambs

There are three main objectives to the management of habitats for conservation: (1) the modification of successional changes in vegetation and its associated fauna; (2) the increase of the biotic diversity, or richness of a habitat; and (3) the conservation of rare or endangered species. The success of each of these rests largely upon the identification and manipulation of those environmental factors currently limiting the populations and communities which are wanted. Examples will be given of research in progress showing how this can aid each of these conservation objectives.

One cannot alter a habitat to encourage one species, or group of species, without this having repercussions on other parts of the flora and fauna. For this reason, there must be a clear understanding of the objectives to be achieved and research into the best way of achieving them, before conservation can be put on a firm scientific basis.

For centuries man has managed natural vegetation for his own ends. The practices of forestry and agriculture have long involved the manipulation of edaphic factors (cultivations, fertilizer applications and liming), together with the control of biotic factors, such as plant competition (by grazing, burning or herbicides). Although management for nature conservation is a relatively recent activity, it has therefore developed from a long history of practical experience of vegetation management (Duffey & Watt 1971).

By comparison, man has far less experience of successful management of wild animals. In fact, his history as a hunter has shown him to be particularly inept at this, since his over-exploitation of prey species has led to the extinction of many of them. Conservation of fauna does not then have the same history of practical experience on which to call, as does the conservation of flora.

Most ecosystems in Britain are to some extent subject to human influences (Pigott 1976). Many are in fact stages in natural successions, stabilized by treatments imposed by man. Frequently, a particular ecosystem may be conserved simply by persisting with a management practice which has been in operation for many years; for example, the grazing of chalk grassland, or the coppicing of woodlands.

It is frequently assumed that if particular assemblages of plants are conserved in this way, the associated fauna will look after itself. There is, however, a growing body of evidence to show that this is not necessarily true. There is a basic difference between plants and animals which needs to be taken into consideration when assessing the objectives of management. Many plant species are extremely long-lived and are capable of vegetative reproduction. This means that for many plants, the individual is the basic unit for conservation. Practical management is therefore frequently aimed at ensuring the persistence of individuals of one species, by manipulating the environment, so as to improve their competitive ability in relation to other species. All but the most primitive of animals depend upon sexual reproduction and for them the unit of conservation is the population, not the individual. For animals, management practices must aim at ensuring that a large enough population persists to be viable. This is, of course, an over-simplification. Some plants are short-lived and depend totally on sexual reproduction, whilst a few species of animal will multiply by vegetative means. However, the generalization is, I believe, a valid one, and it has considerable bearing on the objectives and the limitations of management practices.

Broadly speaking, management of wildlife is aimed at three main objectives. First, the maintenance of stages in the natural succession of vegetation and its associated fauna; secondly, an increase in the biotic diversity or richness of an area; and thirdly, the persistence of individual, rare or local, species. The differing needs of plants and animals puts differing limitations on the value of each of these objectives for their conservation.

One of the main aims of ecological research is to understand the factors determining the presence or absence of particular species, or assemblages of species, in an area. Management for conservation should be based upon the results of such research since only then can it take into account the very different needs of different species. What I hope to do in this paper is to discuss the value of the three main objectives listed above to the conservation needs of different species, as highlighted by recent research.

MAINTENANCE OF STAGES IN NATURAL SUCCESSIONS

The most commonly practised management on nature reserves is aimed at the maintenance of particular assemblages of plants by treatments which limit successional changes. In effect this is the imposition of a static state on a dynamic one, and so its success rests on the identification of those factors which are capable of balancing the natural successional changes. As was pointed out earlier, this frequently involves the maintenance of existing methods of land use, but it is also worth remembering that the continuation of traditional management practices simply maintains a *status quo*. We invariably do not know what has been lost as a result of current land use, nor what would result from any change in management. In my opinion, there is a need for a far more experimental approach to management.

It is sometimes impossible to continue with a traditional method of management. An example of this is seen in the well documented changes which occurred in our chalk grasslands following the dramatic reduction in rabbit numbers due to myxomatosis in the mid-1950s (Thomas 1960, 1963). The subsequent reduction in grazing pressure led to an invasion by scrub and coarse grasses and a loss of those plant species of low competitive ability. Experimental replacement of the rabbit by other grazing animals, or by mechanical cutting, has shown that the floristic richness of chalk grassland can be maintained by management of the vegetation (Wells 1971). The balance of plant species within the sward resulting from cutting differs from that produced by grazing (just as different species of grazers produce different results) but the same plant species persist under both forms of management. This is because chalk grassland is made up predominantly of long-lived plant species that are reproducing primarily by vegetative means. It is sometimes difficult to define what is meant by an individual under these circumstances, since it is uncertain when a daughter plant takes over from its parent, but cutting and grazing lead to a greater persistence of individuals of those species which do not compete well with ranker vegetation. Wells (1973) showed that over 90 % of the plants in his chalk grassland plots were perennials and that these persisted in the closed sward without reproduction by seed. There are few estimates of the longevity of these plants, but what evidence there is suggests that they are extremely long-lived; up to a hundred years or more in some species.

Autecological studies of a number of specific phytophagous insects have shown that the presence of an abundance of their food plant does not necessarily ensure their persistence. Often quite subtle variations in the performance of the plant can determine its acceptability to an insect herbivore. An example of this is seen from my own work on the swallowtail butterfly, *Papilio machaon* (Dempster, King & Lakhani 1976).

At one time this species occurred throughout the East Anglian fens. With the drainage of these, however, much of its habitat was destroyed and it persisted only around the Norfolk Broads and as an isolated population at Wicken Fen, Cambridgeshire. This latter population survived until the early 1950s, when it became extinct, and so far repeated attempts to re-establish the butterfly there have failed. The drainage of the surrounding land has led to an oxidation and shrinkage of the peat soil, so that Wicken Fen is now some 2.5–3.0 m above the surrounding land. This has led to a drying out of the Fen and to an invasion of scrub. The butterfly's food plant, milk parsley (*Peucedanum palustre*), is still locally abundant on the Fen, but its performance is markedly poorer than on the marshes around the Norfolk Broads. At Wicken it is shorter-lived and the individual plants are far smaller. The size of the plants has an important effect on their acceptability to the butterfly. The female swallowtail selects only those parts of the plant exposed above surrounding vegetation on which to lay her eggs. At Wicken few of the plants are large enough in early summer to be found by the egg-laying females. This is entirely due to the dryness of the conditions in which they are living. Wicken and Norfolk plants survived and performed equally well, when grown in a greenhouse at Monks Wood.

In this example, the successional changes in the vegetation occurring as a result of drying of the Fen, affected the butterfly long before its food plant was eliminated. The latter persists at Wicken because the open fen vegetation is now cut regularly, so as to prevent the invasion of scrub. Under these conditions, the plant can maintain its numbers, but it produces few large, long-lived plants which the butterfly needs.

The age and structure of vegetation can have considerable effects on its fauna. For example, although the characteristic flora of chalk grassland may be conserved by cutting, its fauna may become greatly impoverished if the vegetation is kept too short and plants are prevented from flowering. Morris (1971) showed that the greatest diversity of invertebrate animals could be obtained by leaving some areas uncut for a number of years, since some species occur only in either cut or uncut grassland. He therefore recommended the rotational cutting of relatively small areas for maximum conservation value.

Maintenance of diversity

There is often a wish to ensure that nature reserves carry as wide a range of species as possible. Added to this, ecotones, that is transition zones between two habitat types, are often far richer in plant and animal species than either habitat which they separate. This has led to management practices aimed specifically at creating diversity.

Diversity can, of course, be improved by increasing the number of habitat types and by increasing the variability within any one habitat. For example, a uniform, closed canopy woodland is far less rich in species than one containing open clearings. Similarly, woodlands containing trees of a mixed age are richer than single-aged plantations, especially when dead timber is present. The latter is essential for some species of insects, birds and fungi. The different levels at which diversity can be achieved, both within and between habitats, makes it particularly difficult to generalize about its value to conservation.

Many plants can persist as individuals in very small areas. Animals, on the other hand, frequently need large areas of one habitat type to survive. In their study of the fauna juniper (*Juniperus communis*) for example, Ward & Lakhani (in press) showed that the number of native insects occurring on an area of juniper, depends upon the size of the habitat, as measured by the number of plants present. Only on sites which contained over 3000 juniper bushes was there a reasonable expectation of finding the 15 commoner species of phytophagous insects which are restricted to this plant. Vertebrates usually need even larger areas of suitable habitat than invertebrates for their survival. This need for minimal areas for the conservation of different species makes the practice of aiming for a diversity of habitats of doubtful value unless the area of each is large.

Small-scale diversity within any one habitat may, on the other hand, be extremely valuable. We saw an example of this in Morris's study of the fauna of chalk grassland (Morris 1971). Heterogeneity within habitats may well aid the persistence of populations of both animals and plants (den Boer 1968; Dempster 1971), particularly when these are near the edge of their geographical distribution. Small variations within a habitat may buffer the populations against environmental fluctuations, since some individuals may survive extreme conditions in the temporarily more favourable parts of the habitat. For this reason, it is probably inadvisable to manage large areas of habitat in any one way, or at any one time, although there will be minimal areas of the component parts of the habitat which will be needed by different species. Again the limitations of this need to be studied.

THE CONSERVATION OF INDIVIDUAL SPECIES

It is sometimes argued that with the large number of species in our flora and fauna, conservationists can never hope to understand sufficient to make the conservation of individual species practicable. If this is so, it may be better to aim management practices at the broader conservation of ecosystems or communities. I do not accept this, however, because certain types of organism are likely to be lost if such an attitude is adopted. Generally speaking, it will be the more highly specialized species which will be in greatest 'danger of extinction if their needs are not catered for. Some of these are ecologically among the most interesting components of our flora and fauna and some also have a high appeal to the general public.

There is invariably a complex of factors determining the abundance of any one organism and this complex can only be unravelled by a detailed study of the population dynamics of that organism. In my opinion, there is no short-cut to this, since superficial inspection of a species' requirements may be extremely misleading. An example of this can be seen from current research by Dr J. A. Thomas on the rarest of our British butterflies, the large blue (*Maculinea arion*).

The large blue has always been a very local species in Britain, but during the past 20 years, or so, it has declined in abundance so that at present only one small colony is known to exist. Apart from its rarity and the remoteness of the sites where it occurred, the main fascination of this species is its very odd life cycle.

The adult butterflies emerge in late June and the females lay their eggs on the flower buds of thyme, *Thymus drucei*. The eggs hatch in about 10 days and the young caterpillars bore into the old florets and feed on the developing seeds. They continue feeding on thyme until about the middle of August, when they leave the plants. At this stage the caterpillar secretes, from a pair of posterior glands, a sugary liquid which is attractive to ants of the genus *Myrmica*. If found by these ants, the caterpillar is eventually carried back into their underground nests. Here it will spend the rest of its life, feeding on ant grubs. When fully grown, the caterpillar pupates near the surface of the nest and the adult butterfly subsequently crawls to the surface, before inflating its wings. There is only a single generation each year. Dr Thomas has been studying the large blue under contract to the N.C.C. since

1972. Much of his work is still unpublished, but he has kindly allowed me to quote some of his findings.

There is little doubt that the distribution of the large blue has been contracting for a very long time (Spooner 1963). During the past century, changes in land use have resulted in the loss of many areas of suitable habitat for the butterfly. In the early 1950s there were probably in the order of 35 sites in southwest England where the butterfly still occurred. There is now probably only one. This latest decline has coincided with many sites becoming overgrown with scrub as a result of reduced grazing by rabbits, which in turn was the result of the outbreaks of myxomatosis in the mid-1950s. The reduction in rabbit numbers also led to many sites being put over to arable farming. Even so, there are still many sites which look suitable for the species, and contain plenty of its food plants, but where the butterfly no longer occurs. This loss of the butterfly from apparently suitable habitat has led to a large number of theories to account for its decline, ranging from over-collecting, and weather factors, to physical- or genetic-isolation (Benham 1973; Muggleton & Benham 1975). Dr Thomas's work has shown that probably none of these is the main contributory factor to the recent decline. Instead, it is probably a change in the status of its ant hosts that is responsible for the loss of the butterfly.

A detailed population study has been made of the butterfly on its last surviving site. This has shown that the weather during the period of adult life greatly affects the number of eggs laid. As is commonly found with butterflies, cool, cloudy weather reduces their egg-laying activity. Egg mortality is low, but there are often many deaths during early larval life, particularly when densities are high. This is mainly due to cannibalism, and it leads to only one small larva normally surviving on a single flowerhead. The drought in 1975 led to poor flowering of the thyme at the time of egg-laying and this caused high densities of eggs to be laid on those flowers that were present. This resulted in high death-rates from cannibalism in that year.

The highest mortalities occur while the caterpillars are in the ants' nests, and a preliminary analysis of Dr Thomas's data suggests that the key factor determining survival from one generation to the next occurs during the time when the caterpillar is underground.

Four species of *Myrmica* occur commonly in large blue habitats. Of these, two species *M. sabuleti* and *M. scabrinodis* are mainly used as hosts by the large blue. There is some evidence to suggest that *M. sabuleti* is a better host than *M. scabrinodis*, but more work needs to be done on this. A maximum of two adult butterflies has emerged from a single ant nest during this study, although up to six have been recorded in the literature. Of these, three were very small individuals, which was perhaps an indication of starvation when numbers are high. There is little doubt that the food supply of caterpillars, and hence their survival, depends upon the reproductive status of the ant and that this is dependent upon the condition of the habitat. A start has been made to study this experimentally.

A survey of sites where the butterfly recently occurred has shown that *M.*

sabuleti and *M. scabrinodis* are either missing, or at very low densities, on those sites which look superficially to be still suitable for the butterfly. These ants appear unable to survive in the rank vegetation which develops on under-grazed sites. Preliminary results from this study suggest then that the factor limiting survival of the butterfly on these sites is the availability of ant hosts which have thyme plants in their territories.

DISCUSSION AND CONCLUSIONS

The practical management of plants and animals depends upon identifying the factors currently limiting their persistence, either as individuals, populations or communities. This can be achieved only by research into specific conservation problems. The level at which this research is required depends largely upon the mode of life of the organisms in which one is interested. Long-lived, perennial plants, which have the capability of vegetative reproduction, may be conserved as individuals by relatively simple management techniques. It may be necessary to conserve a large number of individuals in order to maintain a reasonable amount of genetic variability, although Parker's work on *Hypochoeris maculata* (Parker 1971) suggests that a high level of heterozygosity may be maintained in very small populations of at least some perennial plants. The conservation of short-lived, sexually reproducing plants, especially in non-ruderal habitats will be more difficult, since their requirements are more akin to those of the majority of animals. For these, the unit of conservation must be the population, and so their requirements can only be discovered by studies of their population dynamics.

Clearly, detailed studies cannot be made for all animals and plants and the first priority must be given to rare or endangered species. These are often highly specialized in their needs and frequently they have poor powers of dispersal. Management of small areas specifically for particularly interesting or valued species is perfectly possible provided enough is known about their ecology. Introductions to new or unoccupied habitats may also prove necessary, if their natural powers of dispersal are low.

For the majority of species, conservation will need to be aimed at communities or ecosystems. At present, virtually all of the management techniques used in conservation are based upon traditional methods of vegetation management. These frequently have limitations in their value for conserving animals and far more research is needed into the maintenance of particular communities of these.

One cannot alter a habitat to encourage one species, or group of species, without this having repercussions on other parts of the flora and fauna. For this reason, there must be a clear understanding as to the objectives to be achieved by management of any particular area. Only then is it worth while doing research into how best these objectives can be achieved and into what impact this will have on other species. This need to define the objectives of wildlife management, both inside and outside reserves, cannot be over-emphasized. In this, local interests must be weighed against wider, national or international interests. There should also be a better balance than at present, between conserving those species which have a wide public appeal (such as birds, mammals and butterflies), and those, less conspicuous, but nonetheless essential components of our flora and fauna. If we were really rational about this, we should perhaps be worrying far more about conservation of the soil micro-flora and fauna, than about survival of the osprey in Scotland.

I am indebted to Dr B. N. K. Davis, Dr M. W. Holdgate, Mr J. N. R. Jeffers, Professor F. T. Last, Dr M. G. Morris, Dr E. Pollard, Dr J. A. Thomas and Mr T. C. E. Wells for their helpful comments on the manuscript.

REFERENCES (Dempster)

Benham, B. R. 1973 The decline (and fall?) of the Large Blue butterfly. *Bull. amat. Ent. Soc.* **32**, 88–94.

Dempster, J. P. 1971 The population ecology of the Cinnabar Moth, *Tyria jacobaeae* L. (Lepidoptera, Arctiidae). *Oecologia* **7**, 26–67.

Dempster, J. P., King, M. L. & Lakhani, K. H. 1976 The status of the swallowtail butterfly in Britain. *Ecol. Entomol.* **1**, 71–84.

den Boer, P. J. 1968 Spreading of risk and stabilization of animal numbers. *Acta biotheor.* **18**, 165–194.

Duffey, E. & Watt, A. S. (ed.) 1971 *The scientific management of animal and plant communities for conservation.* Oxford: Blackwell Scientific Publications.

Morris, M. G. 1971 The management of grassland for the conservation of invertebrate animals. In Duffey & Watt (1971), pp. 527–552.

Muggleton, J. & Benham, B. R. 1975 Isolation and the decline of the Large Blue butterfly (*Maculinea arion*) in Great Britain. *Biol. Conserv.* **7**, 119–128.

Parker, J. S. 1971 The control of recombination. D.Phil. Thesis, University of Oxford.

Pigott, C. D. 1977 The scientific basis of practical conservation: aims and methods of conservation. *Proc. R. Soc. Lond.* B **197**, 59–68 (this volume).

Spooner, G. M. 1963 On causes of the decline of *Maculinea arion* L. (Lep. Lycaenidae) in Britain. *Entomologist* **96**, 199–210.

Thomas, A. S. 1960 Changes in vegetation since the advent of myxomatosis. *J. Ecol.* **48**, 287–306.

Thomas, A. S. 1963 Further changes in vegetation since the advent of myxomatosis. *J. Ecol.* **51**, 151–183.

Ward, L. K. & Lakhani, K. H. 1977 The conservation of juniper. The fauna of food-plant island sites in southern England. *J. appl. Ecol.* **14**, 121–135.

Wells, T. C. E. 1971 A comparison of the effects of sheep grazing and mechanical cutting on the structure and botanical composition of chalk grassland. In Duffey & Watt (1971), pp. 497–515.

Wells, T. C. E. 1973 Botanical aspects of chalk grassland management. In *Chalk grassland: studies on its conservation and management in south-east England* (eds. A. C. Jermy & P. A. Stott), pp. 10–15. Maidstone: Kent Trust for Nature Conservation Special Publication.

Proc. R. Soc. Lond. B. **197**, 77–96 (1977)

Printed in Great Britain

Conservation problems in the future

By A. D. Bradshaw

Department of Botany, University of Liverpool

Change in existing ecosystems is usually considered to damage nature conservation interest. Yet many of the changes that have occurred in the past since woodland was cleared by primitive man have lead to enhanced interest by providing diversity in a wide variety of sub-climax ecosystems. But the ecosystems are sensitive and liable to further change. Many of the local problems of present-day nature conservation stem from this.

But there are also pervasive changes which because they are widespread are leading to wholesale loss of ecosystems and species. They are important not only on a local scale but also in their effects on the totality of wild life. In these circumstances it appears that we will have to change our attitudes and take account not only of areas which we recognize because of their naturalness, but also man-made habitats.

We shall have to consider the *restoration* as faithfully as possible of areas that have been grossly disturbed, the *reintroduction* of species into areas from which they have been lost, and the *creation* of new areas of conservation interest in totally degraded areas such as gravel pits, quarries and even chemical waste heaps.

Some man-made areas are already of considerable interest and value to nature conservation. But others require deliberate modification and the introduction of appropriate species. Some steps have already been taken in this direction, but there is a wealth of further opportunity. Such work will require the application of scientific knowledge to practical ends: in its turn it can provide us with critical information on the subtleties of plant and animal behaviour.

Introduction

In some respects it is presumptuous to look into the future, as it affects nature conservation, particularly because the needs of conservation are determined so much by the social and economic forces which shape our countryside. Who 50 years ago would have predicted the advent of herbicides and their effects on the plant populations of our arable fields, or the eutrophication and devastation of the waters of the Norfolk Broads?

And yet we must look into the future as best we may in order to be prepared for what may come. In conservation, pleas that forecasting is too difficult will be of little help when the conservation account is bankrupt. Those who drafted the Nature Conservancy Council Act 1973 required the Council 'to take account of actual or possible ecological change'. So it is appropriate, perhaps, that the last contribution to this discussion should take this viewpoint, and examine the changes that may occur in the future and the steps that we may need to take to combat them.

Change

Change in ecosystems has been a recurrent theme in all the contributions to this discussion, perhaps mainly because change in existing ecosystems is usually considered to damage their nature conservation value. On this basis a Neolithic conservationist would be disturbed by what he found in Britain today. But once he got used to the fact that radical changes had occurred, he would be fascinated with the resulting richness of our present-day vegetation – in the variety of ecosystems and the variety of species within ecosystems. He would have some glimmerings of this from studying the effects of his own early forest clearances which we can see today in any pollen profile which records the changes (Godwin 1975). On any criterion the advent of agriculture has enhanced the nature conservation interest of the vegetation of this planet. There are of course some examples which are particularly spectacular such as the contrast between the restricted floristic composition of a beechwood on thin calcareous soils and the range of species in the heavily grazed grassland which replaces it as a result of man's activities. Other man-made communities of particular interest and beauty include mowing fen, lowland heath, and lowland hay meadows. The contribution of man to the nature conservation interest of Britain is indicated by the fact that of the *ca.* 800 sites included in the Nature Conservation Review soon to be published by the Nature Conservancy Council and the Natural Environment Research Council approximately 90 % are influenced or determined by man's activities.

Loss

But change can proceed too far. When the calcareous grassland has been modified further by the addition of fertilizers we are presented with an ecosystem of less biological, and aesthetic, interest. It is not however of no interest, because as a simplified system it may be better for studies of productivity (e.g. Spedding 1971) and of plant autecology (e.g. Putwain & Harper 1970).

Perhaps the crucial point comes when the changes proceed to such an extent that the original ecosystem, the climax woodland, is lost altogether or reduced to such an extent that it is liable to damage by excessive human interference, or is too small an area to maintain stable populations of the species within it (Hooper 1971).

The same can also apply to the plagioclimax ecosystems of equal conservation interest which replace it, leading to serious decline in the species associated, for example the Adonis blue (*Lysandra bellargus*) and the silver-spotted skipper (*Hesperia comma*) of calcareous grassland (Heath 1974) or the fritillary (*Fritillaria meleagris*) (figure 1). In Middlesex since Trimen & Dyer published their flora in 1869, no less than 78 species have disappeared (Kent 1975).

The amount of change that has occurred is reflected in the fact that at present

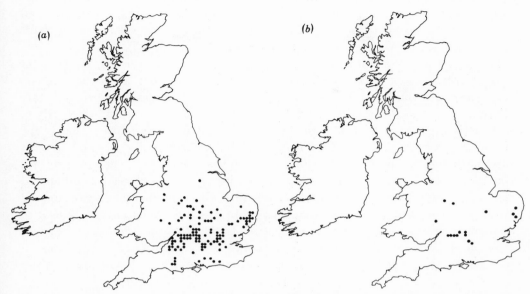

FIGURE 1. The distribution of the fritillary (*Fritillaria meleagris*) in Britain (*a*) before 1930, (*b*) in 1970 (Perring 1974*a*).

only 8 % of the British Isles is covered by deciduous woodland, and of this probably only 20 % is original, covering therefore 1.6 % of our land surface. Other countries of the world are in a better position, but there is no reason for them to be complacent, for the example of countries like Britain where human population numbers grew early is available as a warning.

Two hundred years ago we could have taken comfort from the fact that the semi-natural plagioclimax communities which replaced the woodland were in abundance, for us to enjoy and value. How endless Hardy's Egdon Heath seemed 130 years ago: 'and withal singularly colossal and mysterious in its swarthy monotony'. We know that despite author's licence it was endless compared with what it is today (Moore 1962) (figure 2). Not only has there been a decline in total

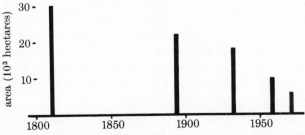

FIGURE 2. The decline in the area of heathland in Dorset from 1800 to the present day (from Moore 1962 and personal communication).

area, but also enormous fragmentation, and the changes are continuing up to the very present. These changes are mirrored throughout the country, and throughout the rest of the world, as the areas ploughed or fertilized have crept ever upwards and species have been progressively eliminated (Perring 1974b).

In some ways the initial forest clearances were not so serious as the later agricultural changes. Little was done to modify soils, so that when the *landnam* phase was over the forest seems to have returned to its apparently original state (Turner 1965), although, as we shall discuss later, it does not return necessarily to its exactly original state. But with the advent of intensive agriculture, firstly the use of lime or marl, and now the use of complete fertilizers, soils have now in most cases been modified permanently. So the Egdon heath that is lost can never return. The permanence of these changes can be seen in any clump of nettles and spread of closely grazed grassland around the derelict hafods or summer holdings of upland Wales, deserted a hundred years ago. In Britain it is true that rainfall will lead to an average annual loss of calcium equivalent to 99 kg/ha Ca (220 lb/acre calcium carbonate) (Cooke 1967), but phosphorus is not readily leached and it can persist in soils for many centuries. At the same time in seral and plagioclimax communities invasion of legumes can cause marked eutrophication (Green 1972).

Maintenance

Against such a background it is essential that we develop systems for preserving what is left. It is obvious, although depressing, that we are not going to be able to stem the tide of agricultural improvement and prevent the use of land of conservation interest for industry, housing and roads. The second Land Utilization Survey has shown how great are the latter pressures, and indeed produces arguments that more wild areas should be brought into agricultural production (Coleman 1976). So it is essential that we have a systematic series of nature reserves, as outlined in the forthcoming Nature Conservation Review. While it may be possible in the future to refine the choice of areas on the basis of more sophisticated methods of survey, the immediate problem is to preserve whatever we can which is of merit, regardless of the perfection of the criteria used. For we are otherwise not going to find enough areas left to retain.

Since such a large proportion of the areas which we would wish to preserve are plagioclimaxes determined by man, and are tied to cultural practices which are fast disappearing, we will have to devise appropriate methods for preserving them. There are a frightening number of areas which have been acquired as representing one or more particular types of community, which do so no longer because of the difficulty of maintaining the original management system. This point is emphasized by the previous contributors to this discussion.

The first step in maintenance must be to devise reliable yet simple methods for monitoring change. Recently there has been a series of discussions on monitoring and surveillance held under the auspices of the Natural Environment Research

Council. But so far we do not have a national system of monitoring for nature conservation purposes: we do not even have a monitoring system for National Nature Reserves. The devising of an effective low-cost system is an interesting challenge for an ecologist with a practical turn of mind as is argued by Dr Hellawell.

The second step is to devise systems of maintenance which do effectively maintain the subtle and obvious characteristics of the area concerned. It may be possible to devise alternative techniques when the original cultural system is no longer possible, such as replacing grazing by mowing on chalk grassland. However, while the replacement techniques do maintain a similar degree of species richness and diversity, the balance in the vegetation does change (Wells 1971). So there may in many cases be no alternative but to maintain the original cultural system. Nevertheless the management of plant and animal communities by alternative means is an important area of research and capable of producing many new insights in the subtleties of population regulation, a subject where our ignorance is profound, as Harper (1971) has argued. But the previous contributors to this discussion meeting have made this amply clear.

Alternative approaches

So far we have been considering ways in which the existing diversity can be maintained. This approach, of *preservation*, is essential. But we should realize that at the moment the National Nature Reserves constitute only 0.5% of the land surface of Gt Britain and the local nature reserves another 0.2%. While we expect these percentages to increase, it is inevitable that most of our wildlife will be outside nature reserves. This will be true everywhere in the world.

Since it is inevitable that, from the point of view of wildlife, the quality and range of the areas outside nature reserves will continue to decline, there will be profound effects on totality of wildlife and even on the viability of the systematic series of nature reserves themselves.

It therefore seems that we must be prepared to consider two other approaches, *restoration* and *creation*, as well. By *restoration* is meant re-establishment of original areas and their ecosystems as faithfully as possible. This so far has not been something that has interested conservationists a great deal, almost certainly because we would not think that it was possible to restore a damaged or destroyed ecosystem to anything approaching its former state. It is obviously difficult to provide a faithful restoration in a short time period, but it is not necessarily impossible in the long term, so long as the essential physical characteristics of the original habitat can be re-established.

By *creation* is meant the establishment of new ecosystems, which although they may well resemble existing or past ecosystems are not necessarily a faithful copy of them. In this approach we would be concerned, using whatever situations became available, to make new areas and communities of nature conservation interest. At first sight this may appear a contradiction, since we usually assume that areas of nature conservation interest are natural, and therefore situations created by us could not be. But the fact that we find so many plagioclimaxes to be of intense value as nature conservation areas completely refutes this argument. Indeed Professor Pigott in this discussion questions the whole basis on which we preserve particular communities and suggests that we should be prepared to replace one ecosystem by another if it is more practicable to maintain the second rather than the first. Elsewhere, Grime (1972) has suggested we must look to man-made areas as the places where wildlife refuges can be made in the future.

These two approaches have a number of different although interrelated aspects which we must consider separately.

RESTORATION

There are a number of situations where restoration is a valid objective. The most important situations are those where there is massive disturbance of the countryside by an extractive industry. This includes a wide range of activities which are having an ever increasing effect on the countryside, often in areas of outstanding conservation interest, such as open-cast mining and quarrying of chalk for cement in this country, and the extraction of rutile and zircon from coastal sands in Australia. But restoration is also needed where there is localized temporary disturbance in an area of conservation interest such as in the laying of a pipeline through moorland or heath. Up to now very few attempts have been made to carry out proper restoration of natural ecosystems, although there is considerable literature on the restoration of a general vegetation cover usually for agricultural use (Goodman & Bray 1975).

Where restoration is for agricultural or general amenity use the original soil can be lost or heavily disturbed because fertility can be restored by the use of lime and fertilizers. The original vegetation can be lost because a new vegetation cover can be sown from commercially available seed whether of agricultural cultivars or other less highly selected material. But in the strict sense this then is not restoration but only reclamation and does not concern us here, except that it teaches us that a creative approach is feasible, and, judging by the amount of research now being carried out, a proper subject for scientific investigation.

Where the original ecosystem is to be faithfully replaced the restoration can be thought of in two steps, firstly the replacement of the original soil system and secondly the replacement of the plant–animal community. In the replacement of the soil system it is necessary to keep the different horizons separate, to store them for as little time as possible or else there will be deterioration of organic matter and soil structure (Hunter & Currie 1956), and to replace them without excessive consolidation. The techniques worked out in relation to open-cast coal mining (by, for example, Knabe 1965, National Coal Board 1974) and sand and gravel extraction (Ministry of Agriculture Fisheries and Food 1971) are applicable, although greater care will be necessary.

The replacement of the original vegetation is where there are greater problems. If the original top soil is respread very quickly as part of a continuous operation a great number of the original species will be carried over in seeds and vegetative material. But shrubs and trees will not be carried over in this manner because their seeds have little or no dormancy. Seed of the appropriate species must therefore be collected and sown. In the restoration carried out by the Australian mineral sands industry who are mining large areas of a rather unique heath vegetation on coastal sands containing a high frequency of members of the Proteaceae, seed-bearing branches of the original vegetation are cut and laid on the restored ground to shed their seed naturally. In this restoration, which is probably the most outstanding of its kind, the vegetation is surveyed before mining and after restoration and if necessary nursery-grown material is planted to restore the populations of individual species to their original frequency. All material comes from the sites and the possibility of genetic differences between populations of individual species allowed for. Since a small loss of plant nutrients, particularly phosphorus, occurs during the disturbance of the soil this is also restored (Coaldrake 1973).

Variations on this technique have been developed in other parts of Australia. At Kambalda, Western Australia, where the original scrub vegetation was destroyed by mining activity but the soil had not been removed, all that has been found necessary is to break up the soil surface by ripping it with deep tines and then to scatter a mulch of broken-up native shrub material which has been passed through a wood chipping machine. The mulch contains the appropriate seeds which germinate readily under the protection of the mulch (J. Vershuer, personal communication).

In this country nothing like this degree of care of restoration has been attempted. But we are now faced with situations such as oil and gas pipeline laying in areas of natural beauty and conservation interest where careful restoration is badly

TABLE 1. SCHEME OF RESTORATION FOR HEATHLAND DOMINATED BY *CALLUNA VULGARIS* WHEN DISTURBED BY PIPE LAYING OPERATIONS (from P. D. Putwain & D. A. Gillham)

1. Adjust state of existing heather – if short, leave – if long, burn or mow with flail and collect mowings
2. Cover area on one side of pipeline with plastic sheet
3. Strip top 100 mm of soil and place on sheet
4. Strip lower soil layers as necessary and keep separate
5. Lay pipe and cover with lower soil layers in sequence without undue compaction
6. Replace top soil with care (including dormant seed and vegetative materials) avoiding unevenness or compaction, as soon as possible (within 7 days)
7.† Supplement seed of *Calluna* (and other species if necessary) by flail mowings or litter collected elsewhere
8.† Oversow with low rate of nurse species *Agrostis tenuis/Festuca ovina* (10–15 kg/ha)
9.† Fertilize with low level of nitrogen and phosphorus (10–20 kg/ha of each)
10. Fence to exclude stock for at least 3 years

  † Adjustment of these items may be necessary to suit individual site conditions.

needed (Moffatt 1975). Investigations by Dr Putwain and Mr Gillham at Liverpool on the reinstatement of moorland dominated by *Calluna vulgaris* show that since the surface 5 cm of the soil profile contains considerable quantities of dormant seed, if this layer is kept separate and not diluted with lower soil layers, a satisfactory re-establishment of *Calluna* is possible. Nutrient levels must be carefully controlled because additions of fertilizer help to stimulate the re-growth of the *Calluna* but may encourage an excessive appearance of rushes (*Juncus effusus*.) The suggested steps in the restoration are given in table 1.

There is no doubt that such techniques are feasible and can if necessary be developed to a sophisticated level which will allow us to restore original ecosystems much more faithfully than we have considered possible in the past.

Reintroduction

Whereas the restoration we have been discussing involves the replacement of whole ecosystems, there is a type of restoration which involves the reinstatement of only a small element of an ecosystem. This is *reintroduction*, where a single species, eliminated because of some past activity no longer operating, is brought back into its original habitat. This is surely a proper activity for conservationists. There seems no logical or philosophical reason why we should not cause change in one direction if we have already caused change in the reverse. Yet there is a definite inexplicable disdain of reintroductions among some people. Zoologists, particularly ornithologists, seem more prepared to make reintroductions than botanists (although quite a lot of unrecorded plant introduction has occurred), perhaps because animals, especially birds, are so mobile that they may reappear in an area unaided, as in the well known case of the avocet (*Recurvirostrata avosetta*) in East England after a period of absence of about 100 years, and others (Sharrock 1974). Plants by contrast have much more fixed distributions which may, as in *Dryas octopetala* and other arctic-alpines, reflect not only present conditions but are also the outcome of various influences at different periods after the glacial period (Godwin 1975). But if the plant becomes eliminated such elegant distribution patterns become rather academic and reintroduction not illogical, particularly when some of the elimination may be due to rapacious plant collectors as in the case of the royal fern (*Osmunda regale*).

If the original habitat remains as it was it would seem simple to reintroduce a species. All that should be necessary is to introduce a sufficient number of individuals to ensure that a satisfactory breeding population is established. In practice reintroductions do not appear to be as easy as this. There are several problems.

Firstly, the habitats which appear to be suitable again for the survival of the species may in fact not be. Thus attempts have been made to establish several of the rarer plant species characteristics of the Breckland of East Anglia outside their present very restricted set of sites without success. In some way the new sites must be unsuitable in some subtle manner. Whether or not other cases of unsuccessful introduction are due to the same cause needs careful examination. In the case of reintroduction of Lepidoptera such as the swallowtail (Dempster, King & Lakhani 1976) the availability of the appropriate food plant in sufficient quantity is a critical factor.

Secondly, since the material of the species available for introduction is alien it may be genetically or phenotypically unadapted to its new environment. This is very obvious in the case of the present very interesting experiments by the Nature Conservancy Council to reintroduce the white-tailed eagle (*Haliaeetus albicilla*) into the island of Rhum. The habitat is completely appropriate, but the birds are being brought half-fledged from northern Norway and are in no way adjusted to their new environment. A great deal of trouble is having to be taken to obtain satisfactory acclimatization, and so far it is not possible to say that this has been achieved but the experiment appears promising. In many reintroductions the genetic characteristics of the introduced material may not be appropriate. In this case a period during which natural selection can cause adaptive genetic changes will have to occur. There is little clear-cut evidence for this, but local population differentiation within species is a well established fact and can certainly in plants lead to considerable loss of fitness when a population is removed from its original habitat into a new one.

Thirdly, there is the problem of establishing sufficient numbers of individuals to form a viable breeding population. In self-fertilizing plants this does not arise, but in animals it is a major problem since there must be sufficient numbers of individuals within the area of reintroduction to maintain a satisfactory minimum population size when the normal population has been reduced by environmental fluctuations. This is one of the major problems in the reintroduction of the large copper butterfly to Woodwalton Fen (Duffey 1968), and has also been emphasized by Dr Dempster.

Despite these problems the reintroduction of species into habitats where they originally occurred can be a successful operation. Indeed introductions and re-introductions of fish have been so successful in Britain that the present pattern of distribution of fish is very confused (Wheeler 1974). From a strict nature conservation standpoint, in the case of fish introduction has been taken too far, although no doubt fishermen would think otherwise. In plants there are innumerable situations where reintroduction could be very valuable. Peterken (1974) has, for instance, drawn attention to the fact that woodlands which are now well established but are in fact secondary may have a reduced herbaceous flora, particularly of species low in mobility characteristic of primary woodland (table 2). Since these species could be threatened by developments in forestry (e.g. Peterken 1976), and because many of them are species of considerable attraction and conservation interest there seems no reason why they should not be reintroduced into selected secondary woodlands areas. Arctic-alpine species, many of whose populations are so fragile and liable to wilful or accidental damage, are another good case for controlled reintroductions into selected areas.

TABLE 2. SPECIES MORE OR LESS CONFINED TO PRIMARY WOODLAND
(from Peterken 1974)

Agropyron caninum	*Luzula pilosa*
Anemone nemorosa	*L. sylvatica*
Aquilegia vulgaris	*Lysimachia nemorum*
Campanula trachelium	*Maianthemum bifolium*
Carex laevigata	*Melampyrum pratense*
C. pallescens	*Melica uniflora*
C. pendula	*Milium effusum*
C. remota	*Neottia nidus avis*
C. strigosa	*Oxalis acetosella*
Chrysosplenium alternifolium	*Paris quadrifolia*
C. oppositifolium	*Platanthera chlorantha*
Convallaria majalis	*Polystichum aculeatum*
Equisetum sylvaticum	*Quercus petraea*
Euonymus europaeus	*Ranunculus auricomus*
Galeobdolon luteum	*Scutellaria galericulata*
Galium odoratum	*Sorbus torminalis*
Hypericum hirsutum	*Tilia cordata*
Lathraea squamaria	*Vicia sylvatica*
Lathyrus montanus	*Viola reichenbachiana*

CREATION

The creation of new habitats is a more radical step. But it is perhaps both easier to effect and on logical analysis more justifiable for conservation. It is easier to effect because there is no need to restore an ecosystem to a determined pre-existing state: all that is necessary is to create an ecosystem of some sort. The only requirement will perhaps be to make one of acceptable nature conservation interest: so the ecosystem of a bare rock face is unlikely to be as acceptable as that of a colonized face.

It is more justifiable because once the new habitat and primary ecosystem has been made we can leave it to develop in its own way, and whatever is produced will be acceptable. Nature conservation has always had to put up with ecological succession and in some situations, particularly hydroseres, this leads to loss of the original open water habitats. So there are several sites where new open water areas have been constructed so that the succession may begin again, e.g. on Wicken Fen.

But if we wanted a concrete example of the value of creating new habitats it is in the comparison of the Cambridgeshire and Norfolk peat fens. The open-cast fuel winning activities of mediaeval man, followed by the need to keep channels open for transport, has produced for us a quite outstanding area of nature conservation interest, the greatest concentration of nature reserves in a single type of habitat anywhere in Britain.

Then a century ago we had a canal-building industry, and today we have a sand and gravel industry. Although these may cause loss of some specialized habitat on rare occasions, they have made, and are making, a great contribution to the diversity of natural habitats in this country. At a time when wetlands are being destroyed by drainage for agriculture and other uses at an alarming rate, the production of new wet areas is of considerable value to nature conservation. In many cases with wise planning, as in the Cotswold Water Park and at the new Empingham Reservoir, a diversity of uses can be achieved so that nature conservation and other activities can co-exist. But time will tell whether these plans are achieved, because open water is of attraction to so many other interests besides nature conservation.

In the same way old quarries, particularly in limestone areas, but in fact widely throughout the country, have become important refuges for wild plants and are now being made into Nature Reserves or Sites of Special Scientific Interest (S.S.S.Is). Their contribution to nature conservation has been shown by Ratcliffe (1974) who points out that 75 out of the total of 3000 S.S.S.Is in this country are quarries and other mineral workings. The floras of these quarries, such as Miller's Dale in the Peak District, and the group in the magnesian limestone in Durham, contain many species of considerable interest (table 3).

TABLE 3. SOME OF THE MORE INTERESTING SPECIES FOUND IN THE MAGNESIAN LIMESTONE QUARRIES OF COUNTY DURHAM (data of B. N. K. Davis)

Acinos arvensis	*Dactylorhiza purpurella*	*Ophioglossum vulgatum*
Anacamptis pyramidalis	*Epipactis atrorubens*	*Ophrys apifera*
Arabis hirsuta	*Erigeron acer*	*Pastinaca sativa*
Astragalus danicus	*Gentianella amarella*	*Plantago maritima*
Blackstonia perfoliata	*Gymnadenia conopsea*	*Salix nigricans*
Botrychium lunaria	*Helianthemum chamaecistus*	*S. pentandra*
Cirsium eriophorum	*Hypericum maculatum*	*S. phylicifolia*
Coeloglossum virida	*H. montanum*	*Sesleria caerulea*
Crepis mollis	*Koeleria cristata*	*Viburnum opulus*
Dactylorhiza praetermissa	*Leontodon taraxacoides*	*Zerna erecta*

But not all these man-made sites are so full of species and have such well developed ecosystems. The process of colonization and ecosystem development take time, whether in wet habitats (e.g. Godwin 1923) or in dry (Locket 1945). Unless we are prepared to wait often at least a life time, we must consider ways in which the processes of development of the ecosystems can be assisted. This can involve both modifications to the habitat and the introduction of species, both of which we must examine.

(a) Habitat modifications

The simplest modification although not necessarily the least expensive is reshaping. This can be purely for aesthetic reasons, to remove awkward rocks or piles of waste material, or for landscape reasons, to give the rock face or lake bank more natural characteristics, or for ecological reasons, to provide a greater variety of habitats. If this shaping is done while the quarry or pit is active, equipment will be available and modifications can be made at low cost.

The scope is enormous. In the construction of the Sevenoaks Gravel Pit Reserve, an imaginative example of the creative approach to nature conservation, islands and bays were formed to give an extended shore line to allow more territory for duck: loafing spots, protected banks, were made to increase the attractiveness to wild fowl. The result has been a higher density of duck than in other comparable areas of water (Harrison 1974). In quarries the rock face can be reshaped to give flatter areas where a greater variety of plants can establish: if the shaping is done carefully these can be made inaccessible to sheep and even other grazing animals. In overburden or waste heaps, such as the sand heaps produced in such abundance by the china clay industry, a whole range of shapes are possible, including steep slopes which will remain in a juvenile state because of erosion, and flatter areas where conditions are more favourable to plant growth.

The establishment of vegetation on new substrates depends on the development of satisfactory physical and nutritional characteristics in the material. This can be seen in natural successions, for instance on glacial moraines (Crocker & Major 1955), or in the artificial establishment of vegetation on industrial materials, for instance on china clay wastes (Bradshaw, Dancer, Handley & Sheldon 1975). In general the over-riding factor is plant nutrients, especially nitrogen and phosphorus. Without adequate nutrients plants cannot grow properly and the establishment of proper root systems essential for survival in drought or other times of physical stress is delayed (Fitter & Bradshaw 1974). But the physical characteristics of the substrate will be compounded with the nutrient characteristics and are also important (Richardson & Greenwood 1967).

There may therefore be a need to ameliorate both the chemical and physical characteristics of the substrate in order to obtain satisfactory conditions for the establishment and growth of the species which it would be desirable to have in the area. The exact levels of amelioration will depend on the site and the requirements. The relationship between the use of nutrients and the floristic composition of grassland has been discussed by Rorison (1971): the same principles apply to a new substrate.

It is sometimes held that any amelioration, especially of nutrients, will lead to a reduction in the number of species that will invade since there will be excessive competition from fast growing grasses and other species. This is of course true if the amount of amelioration is excessive. But two points must be borne in mind: firstly, there will be a considerable loss of nutrients, both initially and subsequently, by leaching: secondly, the effect of even a fairly substantial amount of amelioration will usually lead to levels of nutrients in the substrate much less than those in normal soils (figure 3).

We need to know a great deal more about the amount of amelioration needed to achieve conditions suitable for plant growth in these newly created environments. It is apparent that in wet gravel pits little or no amelioration is necessary because the supplies of water and nutrients are adequate for the aquatic and fen vegetation that invades. But in limestone quarries, for instance, there is little invasion by

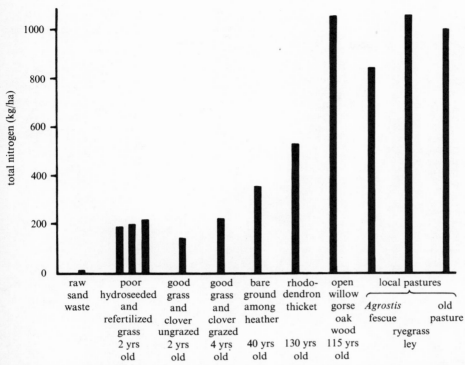

FIGURE 3. The accumulation of nitrogen in the soil in reclaimed and naturally vegetated areas on china clay waste in Cornwall (from Bradshaw, Dancer, Handley & Sheldon 1975).

plants without some amelioration. How much this should be is difficult to predict without resort to field experiments, such as those being carried out by Mr R. N. Humphries in a limestone quarry in Derbyshire. These are designed to see what sort of readily available materials could be used to act as a carrier and a nutrient rich mulch for seeds of a standard set of tree and herb species, to enable species to establish on the quarry face itself. The seed-containing mulches were poured down the face and allowed to run into cracks and crevices. The results at the end of two years (table 4) are encouraging, since the species have endured two very severe droughts. Where the mulch landed in crevices the species have rooted deeply into them. The mulch with highest nutrient content, the mushroom compost, caused the grass to exert very strong competition in the first year, but subsequently it has degraded, and species germinating in the second year such as ash (*Fraxinus excelsior*) are becoming established.

Further experiments are being carried out on the quarry floor using factorial combinations of different levels of organic matter, clay and limestone gravel, and a complex mixture of native and agricultural herbaceous species, to determine minimal levels of amelioration conducive to the growth of desirable native species.

TABLE 4. ESTABLISHMENT OF PLANTS ON LIMESTONE QUARRY FACE (SHELF AREA) AFTER TREATMENT WITH 3 DIFFERENT SEED-CONTAINING MULCHES ONE YEAR PREVIOUSLY (data of R. N. Humphries)

	seed number per square metre in original seeds mixture	sewage sludge	soil	mushroom compost
total vegetation cover		55	40	70
bryophyte cover		15	50	
herbage height (cm)		5–30	5–16	5–40
species cover				
Festuca rubra, *F. ovina*	2800	10	5	5
Lolium perenne	300	20	15	60
Dactylis glomerata	1150	20	5	10
Poa pratensis	50	+	+	
Agrostis tenuis	250			+
Phleum pratense	50		+	+
Cynosurus cristatus	50		+	+
Trifolium pratense	100	1	5	(+)
T. repens	150	1	10	+
Medicago sativa	50	+	+	
Vicia sativa	50	(+)	(+)	(+)
Onobrychis viciifolia	50	+	+	
Lotus corniculatus	100		+	
Quercus robur	1	(+)	(+)	
Rosa canina	40	+	+	(+)
Fraxinus excelsior	19	+	+	+
Crataegus monogyna	6	+	+	
Acer campestre	19	+	+	+
Viburnum opulus	14			
Sorbus aucuparia	1			

+ Present in small numbers.   (+) Present in first summer but not subsequently.

This sort of experiment requires extending to a wider variety of native species and to a variety of sites in different situations. It can equally be extended to other calcareous substrates such as chalk where physical conditions are not so extreme and simple additions of nutrients may be sufficient amelioration. In this way we can obtain a picture of the practical requirements of individual species for their establishment. At the same time it will indicate other more sophisticated experiments to examine the behaviour of individual species, following the example of Lloyd & Pigott (1967), Jeffrey (1971) and others.

The aim in the end will be to carry out modifications which will provide habitats suitable for the desired ecosystem. There will therefore be a considerable element of choice. In most cases however it would seem best to provide a variety of different habitats including those where no amelioration has been carried out, to maintain diversity within the site. In this way the unfortunate situation of a single overall treatment which turned out to be inimicable to particular desired species would not occur. But attention would have to be paid to the size of the component habitats of the site so that they were sufficient to maintain viable populations of individual species.

(b) *Introductions*

In these new sites we can carry out suitable habitat modifications and then leave colonization to occur naturally. In many situations where there is an ample source of species in the vicinity this may work extremely well, and the process of colonization may provide information of considerable biological interest not easily obtainable in normal habitats. However in many situations the numbers and species diversity of suitable seed parents may be inadequate. This is very often the case in the larger and potentially more valuable man-made sites. As a result the vegetation may develop only slowly and become composed of only very few species, into which other later arrivals can invade only with difficulty.

In which case there seems no reason why species should not be introduced on purpose. Such introductions could be either a minimum, involving just a few obviously appropriate species, or a maximum, involving a wide variety of possibly appropriate species both common and rare. The main value of the first course of action is that it will allow a generally appropriate vegetation to be established which can then provide habitats for appropriate animal species. But it will not provide much of botanical interest. The second course of action seems perfectly acceptable, and could lead to a rich diverse flora and fauna.

Since quarries and other similar habitats can be refuges for local and interesting plants such as *Ophrys apifera, O. muscifera, Herminium monorchis, Gentianella germanica* and *G. amarella* (Ratcliffe 1974) why should not similar sites be developed as reserves for a wide variety of species, including those which are extremely rare? Since the habitats are not natural in the first instance many of the philosophical arguments disappear. There are many attempts to retain our rare species in cultivation in Botanic Gardens, but these are fraught with difficulties, not only of loss but also of genetic change by natural selection or hybridization. A semi-natural situation is much more appropriate. The range of species that might be established in a limestone quarry in Derbyshire is given in table 5. There are no doubt others which could be considered. The quarry in which all these species could be found would be a remarkable addition to our range of nature reserves.

Practical science would be involved, to find out how to fit the species into the habitat and how to modify the habitat to fit the species. But there is no doubt that successful introduction is possible. Rawes & Welch (1972), having modified the present-day habitats at Moor House National Nature Reserve by fencing (and thereby created effectively new habitats), have demonstrated that the introduction of a variety of important rare species is possible and that they can become properly established (table 6).

TABLE 5. SOME OF THE SPECIES WHICH COULD BE INTRODUCED INTO A LIME-
STONE QUARRY IN THE PEAK DISTRICT (observations of R. N. Humphries)

species already found in Miller's Dale quarry (total 81)

common species (examples only given)	local or rare species	other species found on lime-stone in the Peak District which are local or rare
Acer pseudoplatanus	*Aira praecox*	*Asplenium viride*
Carex flacca	*Botrychium lunaria*	*Carex digitata*
Corylus avellana	*Dactylorhiza fuchsii*	*C. ornithopoda*
Crataegus monogyna	*Daphne mezereum*	*Cirsium acaulon*
Festuca rubra	*Galium sterneri*	*C. heterophyllum*
Fragaria vesca	*Listera ovata*	*Cynoglossum officinale*
Fraxinus excelsior	*Ophioglossum vulgatum*	*Dianthus deltoides*
Geranium robertianum	*Ophrys apifera*	*Epipactis atrorubens*
Hieracium pilosella	*Orchis macula*	*Gagea lutea*
Leontodon hispidus	*Parnassia palustris*	*Helleborus viridis*
Linum catharticum	*Primula veris*	*Hornungia petraea*
Origanum vulgare	*Prunus padus*	*Orobanche purpurea*
Prunella vulgaris	*Saxifraga tridactylites*	*Potentilla tabernaemontani*
Salix caprea	*Thalictrum minus*	*P. crantzii*
Teucrium scorodonia	*Viburnum opulus*	*Silene nutans*
Thymus drucei		*Thelypteris robertiana*
Trisetum flavescens		

In a quarry or other similarly open site it is possible to adopt a more *laissez-faire* approach. If a variety of different habitats was created in the site, the species to be introduced could then be scattered at random and allowed to establish naturally in the situations which are suitable to the individual species. This would be preferable to a gardening type of approach and could yield information of considerable biological interest.

In all these situations it is to be presumed that the fauna would invade naturally because of its mobility. But in those cases where the species are immobile there is no reason why they should not be introduced in the same manner as the flora.

TABLE 6. SPECIES SUCCESSFULLY ESTABLISHED ON THE MOOR HOUSE NATIONAL
NATURE RESERVE, WESTMORLAND (from Rawes & Welch 1972)

Carex capillaris	*Salix phylicifolia*
Draba incana	*S. reticulata*
Hypericum pulchrum	*Saussurea alpina*
Luzula sylvatica	*Saxifraga aizoides*
Poa alpina	*S. oppositifolia*
Polygonum viviparum	*Sedum rosea*
Polystichum lonchitis	*Sesleria caerulea*
Potentilla crantzii	*Solidago virgaurea*
Salix arbuscula	*Thalictrum alpinum*
S. caprea	*Vaccinium uliginosum*

Where the aim of the site is particularly to encourage animals and the plants are secondary there is no reason why the plants should not be chosen particularly because of their food value and attractiveness to the animals. This has been done for water fowl with conspicuous success in the Sevenoaks Reserve (Harrison 1974).

(c) Special areas

There are some man-made sites in Britain which hardly bear any resemblance to natural habitats but are of potential scientific and conservation value. These are the chemical and mine waste heaps left by industry. Often they are toxic from high concentrations of salts or heavy metals, or are extreme in pH. At one time they were sites which could hardly have been thought to interest ecologists, yet we now see them as sites of great scientific and conservation interest. Not only does their simplicity and extreme nature allow us to test ecological and evolutionary principles more easily, but their flora and fauna is often interesting or even provoking.

The small area of lead/zinc waste at Trelogan, North Wales, for instance, has been considered in 16 scientific papers in the last 20 years, which is quite a reasonable score for an area not more than 100 m × 400 m covered with rubbish and a depauperate flora, and which is not even an S.S.S.I. Its interest lies in the evolutionary processes occurring on it.

Other sites are interesting for the flora they possess. Metalliferous wastes can have a curious flora containing *Thlaspi alpestre*, *Minuartia verna*, *Cochlearia alpina* and *Viola lutea* and other species. Why such a collection of species should come together on a lead/zinc mine is difficult to understand, but recent work (Gartside & McNeilly 1974) on copper mines suggests the main determinant is the ability to evolve metal tolerance.

TABLE 7. SPECIES UNCOMMON IN SOUTH LANCASHIRE AND GREATER MANCHESTER FOUND ON INDUSTRIAL WASTE HABITATS (Gemmell & Greenwood 1977)

Carlina vulgaris	*Erigeron acer*
Centaurium erythraea	*Gymnadenia conopsea*
Dactylorhiza incarnata	*Linum catharticum*
D. purpurella ⎫	*Sisyrinchium bermudiana*
D. fuchsii ⎬ and hybrids	
D. praetermissa ⎭	

In South Lancashire and Greater Manchester there a variety of alkaline wastes, including Leblanc waste, gas lime, and blast furnace slag. These have a rather curious flora of alkaline tolerant common species, but also a number of orchids and other species rare in the general region (table 7). These species are not only attractive in themselves and form communities of considerable interest but also raise problems of their origin. Since the *Dactylorhiza* sp. are forming hybrid swarms there are also evolutionary problems to be investigated (Gemmell & Greenwood 1977).

Several of these areas of industrial waste have attracted sufficient attention to become nature reserves, such as the Plumley Reserve in Cheshire on lime waste from the Solvay process, and the Upton Warren Reserve in Worcestershire formed by subsidence of salt workings and therefore rather saline.

These are all areas which are interesting in their present state. They need to be preserved as wild habitats and not fall victims to the present enthusiasm for reclamation, as Kelcey (1975) has argued. They will bring their own management problems (Gemmell & Crombie 1975). They are also capable of further development by the introduction of other species which cannot overcome the barrier of geographical isolation. They are habitats of considerable potential from both conservation and scientific points of view.

CONCLUSIONS

A creative approach to conservation problems does not mean that we should cease in our efforts to preserve the natural and semi-natural plant and animal communities we already possess. These are sites of immense importance from aesthetic, conservation and scientific points of view. They are the store of our wildlife and the source of our scientific standards.

But inevitably the range and quantity of these areas will continue to decrease and we must look to other areas to provide similar functions. These new areas produced by mining and other industrial activities may in some cases already be valuable areas from a nature conservation standpoint. But in many cases their youth and physical characteristics may make them of little value in their present state.

There seems no reason why we should not take these raw areas, and modify them so that they become areas of nature conservation value and scientific interest. The challenge is considerable because so much of the land surface of this country has been disturbed by man's activities, and we have been left with so many simplified ecosystems.

At the same time we should consider creating diversity in the existing ecosystems which we have modified or simplified by our own activities. We could add considerable interest to our large areas of coniferous woodlands if pockets of deciduous trees with their associated ground flora could be added. We could add variety to upland areas and safeguard some of our rarer species if we had a policy of introduction and reintroduction in selected mountain sites. We could increase considerably the diversity and interest of some of our intensively used amenity areas such as parks and open spaces by carefully planned modifications and introduction. We could take over selected areas of lowland grassland and similar areas and provide a systematic management together with a carefully planned series of introductions to make refuges for our fast vanishing lowland grassland flora and fauna, for instance in the Breckland (Watt 1971).

This policy is being adopted with conspicuous success in a number of situations. These examples should encourage further developments. At first sight it may seem to be a policy more to do with the application of science than with science itself. But indeed it demands a great deal of careful science to discover what is possible, and it can contribute a great deal to science in revealing the subtleties of plant and animal behaviour which only become apparent in the acid test of whether or not the required species can actually be grown successfully. And it has an essential attribute of science, that it is creative.

In preparing this account I have had a great deal of help from many friends and colleagues, particularly within my own Department and within the Nature Conservancy Council. I am very grateful to them, and in particular to those who have allowed me to use their unpublished data, who are indicated in the text.

REFERENCES (Bradshaw)

Bradshaw, A. D., Dancer, W. S., Handley, J. F. & Sheldon, J. C. 1975 The biology of land revegetation and the reclamation of the china clay wastes in Cornwall. In *The ecology of resource degradation and renewal* (eds M. J. Chadwick & G. T. Goodman). *Br. Ecol. Soc. Symp.* **15**, 363–384.

Coaldrake, J. E. 1973 Conservation problems of coastal sand and open-cast mining. In *Nature conservation in the Pacific* (ed. C.S.I.R.O.), pp. 299–314. Canberra: Australian National University Press.

Coleman, A. 1976 Is planning really necessary? *Geog. J.* **142**, 411–437.

Cooke, G. W. 1967 *The control of soil fertility.* London: Crosby Lockwood.

Crocker, R. L. & Major, J. 1955 Soil development in relation to vegetation and surface age at Glacier Bay, Alaska. *J. Ecol.* **43**, 427–448.

Dempster, J. P., King, M. L. & Lakhani, K. H. 1976 The status of the swallowtail butterfly in Britain. *Ecol. Entomol.* **1**, 71–84.

Duffey, E. 1968 Ecological studies on the Large Copper Butterfly *Lycaena dispar* Haw. *batavus* Obth. at Woodwalton Fen National Nature Reserve. *J. appl. Ecol.* **5**, 69–96.

Fitter, A. H. & Bradshaw, A. D. 1974 Root penetration of *Lolium perenne* on colliery shale in response to reclamation treatments. *J. appl. Ecol.* **11**, 609–616.

Gartside, D. W. & McNeilly, T. 1974 The potential for evolution of heavy metal tolerance in plants. II. Copper tolerance in normal populations of different plant species. *Heredity* **32**, 335–348.

Gemmell, R. P. & Crombie, A. S. 1975 Management of waste tips for enhancement of landscape quality. *Landscape Res. News* **1.11**, 10–11.

Gemmell, R. P. & Greenwood, E. A. 1977 The significance of industrial habitats for wild life conservation. In preparation.

Godwin, H. 1923 Dispersal of pond floras. *J. Ecol.* **11**, 160–164.

Godwin, H. 1975 *History of the British flora,* 2nd ed. London: Cambridge University Press.

Goodman, G. T. & Bray, S. 1975 *Ecological aspects of the reclamation of derelict and disturbed land.* Norwich: Geo Abstracts.

Green, B. H. 1972 The relevance of seral eutrophication and plant competition to the management of successional communities. *Biol. Conserv.* **4**, 378–384.

Grime, J. P. 1972 The creative approach to nature conservation. In *The future of man* (eds F. J. Ebbing & G. W. Heath). *Inst. Biology Symp.* **20**, 47–54.

Harper, J. L. 1971 Grazing, fertilisers, and pesticides in the management of grasslands. In *The scientific management of animal and plant communities for conservation* (ed. Duffey, E. & Watts, A. S.). *Symp. Br. Ecol. Soc.* **11**, 15–31.

Harrison, J. 1974 *The Sevenoaks Gravel Pit Reserve.* Chester: WAGBI.

Heath, J. 1974 A century of change in the Lepidoptera. In *The changing flora and fauna of Britain* (ed. D. L. Hawksworth), pp. 275–292. London: Academic Press.

Hooper, M. D. 1971 The size and surroundings of nature reserves. In *The scientific management of animal and plant communities for conservation* (eds E. Duffey & A. S. Watt). *Symp. Br. Ecol. Soc.* **11**, 555–562.

Hunter, F. & Currie, J. A. 1956 Structural changes during bulk soil storage. *J. Soil Sci.* **7**, 75–80.

Jeffrey, D. W. 1971 The experiment alteration of a *Kobresia*-rich sward in Upper Teesdale. In *The scientific management of animal and plant communities for conservation* (eds E. Duffey & A. S. Watt). *Symp. Br. Ecol. Soc.* **11**, 79–89.

Kelcey, J. G. 1975 Industrial development and wildlife conservation. *Environ. Conserv.* **2**, 99–108.

Kent, D. H. 1975 *The historical flora of Middlesex.* London: The Ray Society.

Knabe, W. 1965 Observations on world wide efforts to reclaim industrial waste land. In *Ecology and the industrial society* (ed. G. T. Goodman). *Symp. Br. Ecol. Soc.* **5**, 263–296.

Lloyd, P. S. & Pigott, C. D. 1967 The influence of soil conditions on the course of succession on the chalk of southern England. *J. Ecol.* **55**, 137–146.

Locket, G. H. 1945 Observations on the colonisation of bare chalk. *J. Ecol.* **33**, 205–209.

Ministry of Agriculture, Fisheries & Food 1971 *The restoration of sand and gravel workings.* London: M.A.F.F.

Moffatt, J. D. 1975 Pipeline installation: problems, effects and improvements. *Landscape Design* **112**, 29–31.

Moore, N. W. 1962 The heaths of Dorset and their conservation. *J. Ecol.* **50**, 369–392.

National Coal Board 1974 *Open cast operations* 1. London: National Coal Board. Open Cast Executive.

Perring, F. H. 1974a Changes in our native vascular plant flora. In *The changing flora and fauna of Britain* (ed. D. L. Hawksworth), pp. 7–25. London: Academic Press.

Perring, F. H. 1974b The last seventy years. In *The flora of a changing Britain* (ed. F. Perring), pp. 128–135. Faringdon, Berks: Classey.

Peterken, G. F. 1974 A method of assessing woodland flora for conservation using indicator species. *Biol. Conserv.* **6**, 239–245.

Peterken, G. F. 1976 Long term changes in the woodlands of Rockingham Forest and other areas. *J. Ecol.* **64**, 123–146.

Putwain, P. D. & Harper, J. L. 1970 Studies on the dynamics of plant populations. III. The influence of associated species on populations of *Rumex acetosa* L. and *R. acetosella* in grassland. *J. Ecol.* **58**, 251–64.

Ratcliffe, D. 1974 Ecological effects of mineral exploitation in the United Kingdom and their significance to nature conservation. *Proc. R. Soc. Lond.* A **339**, 355–372.

Rawes, M. & Welch, D. 1972 Trials to recreate floristically-rich vegetation by plant introduction in the Northern Pennines, England. *Biol. Conserv.* **4**, 135–140.

Richardson, J. A. & Greenwood, E. F. 1967 Soil moisture tension in relation to the colonisation of pit heaps. *Proc. Univ. Newcastle Philosoph. Soc.* **1**, 129–136.

Rorison, I. H. 1971 The use of nutrients in the control of the floristic composition of grassland. In *The scientific management of animal and plant communities for conservation* (eds E. Duffey & A. S. Watt). *Symp. Br. Ecol. Soc.* **11**, 65–77.

Sharrock, J. T. R. 1974 The changing status of breeding birds in Britain and Ireland. In *The changing flora and fauna of Britain* (ed. D. L. Hawksworth), pp. 203–220. London: Academic Press.

Spedding, C. W. 1971 *Grassland ecology.* London: Oxford University Press.

Turner, J. 1965 A contribution to the history of forest clearance. *Proc. Roy. Soc. Lond.* B **161**, 343–354.

Watt, A. S. 1971 Rare species in Breckland: their management for survival. *J. appl. Ecol.* **8**, 593–609.

Wells, T. C. E. 1971 A comparison of the effects of sheep grazing and mechanical cutting on the structure and botanical composition of chalk grassland. In *The scientific management of animal and plant communities for conservation* (eds E. Duffey & A. S. Watt). *Symp. Br. Ecol. Soc.* **11**, 497–515.

Wheeler, A. 1974 Changes in the freshwater fish fauna of Britain. In *The changing flora and fauna of Britain* (ed. D. L. Hawksworth), pp. 157–178. London: Academic Press.

Proc. R. Soc. Lond. B. **197**, 97–99 (1977)

Printed in Great Britain

General discussion

V. C. WYNNE-EDWARDS (*Department of Zoology, University of Aberdeen*). In opening the final discussion the Chairman said we had heard a great deal about the value of science to nature reserves, but what are the values of nature reserves to science?

In giving an example of this, may I begin by taking up a remark made a few minutes ago by Professor Bradshaw about the quick effects to be expected of natural selection, in protecting the gene-pools of native trees and other plants in nature reserves from adulteration by allochthonous strains of the same species, if these were introduced to the reserves from elsewhere. Let me remind you that not all the effects of natural selection are equally rapid in suppressing non-adaptive genes. The selective advantage or disadvantage of some mutations may not be put to the test for many generations. If this were not so, and if selection could only result in maximizing the fitness of the individual in the short term, then the evolutionist could not explain the origin of 'prudential' adaptations, such as those that control population density and population growth in many animals. These usually involve altruistic responses, that is to say, the sacrifice of individual advantage for the long-term benefit of the group. How such delayed selection actually takes effect is still imperfectly understood; and because it involves long time-scales our only hope of investigating it is in ecosystems that have lain long undisturbed, for centuries at least, and dynamic equilibria established.

Increasingly, such conditions are becoming confined to nature reserves in old-established stable ecosystems. Really primeval ecosystems have been and are being severely diminished in extent, most seriously of all in the species-rich tropical zone. The retention of adequate samples of them as reserves is of great importance to science, for reasons of which this is but one illustration.

M. G. MORRIS (*Furzebrook Research Station (I.T.E.), Wareham, Dorset*). It is unreal and misleading to ask the question 'What has nature conservation achieved for science?' Science exists to describe the universe *as it is* and takes no account of what we, as conservationists, have done, feebly, to alter our small part of it. The value judgements which we necessarily take, we take as conservationists. As scientists we describe, measure and predict. We must be clear which rôle we play at any particular time. It is only because the scientist and conservationist are combined in one individual that the question of value judgements being given by a scientist ever arises.

C. D. PIGOTT (*University of Lancaster, Department of Biological Sciences, Lancaster, LA1 4YQ*). Conservation does have a direct contribution to science. It is within natural ecosystems that almost all species have evolved. The nature of vegetation and the mechanisms of competition and natural selection are amenable to strict analytical and experimental studies. The investigation of the complexity of these natural systems requires as strict a scientific discipline as does, for example, the study of nuclear physics. For this work it is essential to have examples of natural ecosystems and often to have them secure from destruction or interference for long-term investigations and future study.

D. A. RATCLIFFE (*Nature Conservancy Council, London*). Nature reserves have been variably used for research, which has included both work aimed to elicitate management techniques and that intended to advance basic scientific knowledge. The Moor House N.N.R. is a good example, as one which has been used extensively by Nature Conservancy and university scientists for studies of the blanket bog and upland river ecosystems, including especially work on nutrient budgets, primary and secondary production, catchment hydrology and stream flow, and growth of species under marginal conditions. These have contributed significantly to the I.B.P. tundra biome work, now synthesized and published.

K. MELLANBY (*President, Bedfordshire and Huntingdon Naturalists Trust, and member of the National Executive, Council for the Protection of Rural England*). Conservationists, concerned with protecting the native flora and fauna of Britain, should be more aggressive and less apologetic. They should not try to justify conservation, as had Professor Harley, because ecological work in applied biology was, potentially, of economic importance. Conservation could be adequately justified on scientific, educational, cultural, aesthetic, recreational and (even) sentimental grounds, as indicated by Dr Ratcliffe. It was suggested that it was wrong to wish to set aside land for nature reserves, or where conservation had priority, because of our growing population and the need to produce more food. There was at present little real conflict between farming and conservation. Since 1945 we had lost about 400 000 ha (one million acres) of good farmland to building, factories, road and airports. In the same period National Nature Reserves and other conservation areas had taken less than 200 000 ha (half a million acres), but only a tiny fraction of this was grade 1 or grade 2 farm land, most was much less productive. We should concentrate on saving farm land from being swallowed up at the present rate of 32 000 ha (80 000 acres) a year for urban and industrial development.

Britain is not, in fact, yet short of land to grow food. I have demonstrated in a book *Can Britain feed itself?* that we already produced enough to give all our population a complete (if dull) diet. We were short of land because we enjoyed eating more meat than we needed (or, possibly, was good for us). If we could persuade our population to be less carnivorous, we could produce all the food we needed and still set aside more land for conservation. Our immediate goal should be 100 000 ha (250 000 acres) of good farmland, and at least a further 400 000 ha (one million acres) of poor land, for conservation reserves. Only with adequate land would it be possible to apply the results of scientific research on conservation.

D. L. HAWKSWORTH (*Commonwealth Mycological Institute, Ferry Lane, Kew, Surrey TW9 3AF*). One aspect we have not considered at this meeting is taxonomy. As is evident from *The changing flora and fauna of Britain* (ed. D. L. Hawksworth, 1974), the state of our knowledge of different groups of plants and animals varies enormously; some are well-known while others are relatively untouched with species new to the British Isles being discovered or rediscovered apace. Dr Ratcliffe, in his contribution this morning, pointed out that the initial survey (primarily a taxonomic exercise) was a fundamental part of the procedure for determining which sites merit conservation. At the present time, however, no single S.S.S.I. or N.N.R. appears to have been thoroughly surveyed from the standpoint of determining its total species composition, notwithstanding the important steps towards this end taken in *Monks Wood* (eds R. C. Steele & R. C. Welch, 1973) and *Hayley Wood* (ed. O. Rackham, 1975). While we can already state that a particular site is of scientific importance for one or more reasons arising from studies which have been carried out, to me an incomplete data-base makes meaningful discussions of both the diversity (in terms of the species content of all groups) and relative importance of such sites somewhat premature at present.

While these considerations are perhaps taken somewhat for granted by many of the participants in this meeting, I feel that the need for increased taxonomic survey work, at the very least in our National Nature Reserves, should not be under-estimated.

Proc. R. Soc. Lond. B. **197**, 101–103 (1977)
Printed in Great Britain

Concluding remarks

By R. E. Boote
Director, Nature Conservancy Council

I would like to end today's discussion in a wider context. This year, after an absence of three years, I returned actively to international conservation. I attended the Conference of European Ministers for the Environment in March and now serve on the Board of the International Union for the Conservation of Nature. This work has sharply reinforced two main impressions or value judgements that have been forming in my mind from the home front.

The first is that many of the aims we nature conservationists strove for in the 1960s have now been accepted by Governments and peoples in Europe and are in process of being realized – pesticide control, safeguarding sites, environmental education, international conventions for wildlife and so on.

My second impression is that we need now urgently to be developing a new thrust for policy and action for the 1980s and beyond, but I cannot find the purpose, drive and élan which characterized the 1960s – a lot of which came from scientists who were not acting *sensu stricto* as ecologists but operating with their hearts and minds as conservationists. And I must emphasize that conservationists – as distinct from scientists qua scientists – are concerned with actions and policies.

On my first value judgement – to realize and improve on our agreed aims in the U.K. and in the rest of Europe – we require much better use of existing knowledge as well as much more knowledge as Professor Harley, Drs Ratcliffe and Dempster so clearly state.

In fact, I believe we are not yet using effectively the knowledge we have. Despite Professor Thorpe's reference to the wealth of material in scientific and other journals, too little is in a usable form for the decision maker, the professional and the operative. We have also, I believe, been living for too long on past capital knowledge. As Dr Hellawell shows, we need much better systems to respond to the trends and changes and increasing pressures on the natural environment. And we must increasingly seek out the opportunities to experiment, restore and create new quality in our surroundings and develop our scientific abilities to do this, as urged by Professors Pigott and Bradshaw.

On the world scale, as you will know, the great theme is now eco-development. I.U.C.N. defines this as development of the oikos, the home or locality – making the fullest sustainable use of the locality's resources and of the knowledge, attitudes techniques, technologies and other adaptations of the local people to their locality. This emphasis on locality reflects the obvious though hitherto neglected fact that environments and their inhabitants differ substantially throughout the world, and that such differences present both problems and opportunities which require special responses.

But this approach, too, will not succeed unless poverty and faulty distribution of resources are soon remedied. The recent United Nations Conference on Trade and Development clearly revealed that the poorer countries are not going to accept and work to conservation goals unless they see that these are relevant to their survival in decent conditions. And the Habitat Conference confirms that if we in the developed countries do not think and act in ways which are going to knit together the people and physical fabric and resources of our one biosphere, then we shall find that the pressures on our land for more minerals and for more food and timber production will become even greater. The climate of world opinion in which to achieve this would deteriorate. And nature conservation goals will be more difficult to achieve.

So, turning to the question of the new thrust for the 1980s and beyond, I suggest that we must relate scientifically-based nature conservation everywhere to the major basic functions of man affecting the natural environment – agriculture, forestry, water and mineral exploitation and so on. This is vital if we are to conserve nature in the ways talked of today, both narrowly and widely; if we are to avoid the natural environment being used up; and the scarce and irreplaceable going for ever.

To achieve this, both at home and abroad, needs much greater penetration into ecological factors and trends. As my colleague Dr Ratcliffe, the N.C.C.'s Chief Scientist, has explained, my Council has contracted a significant part of its research effort to these goals. And we have currently in preparation discussion papers on nature conservation and these major functions which will, I believe, provide a new basis for national action.

But today's meeting is about the scientific aspects of nature conservation and these must include the need for much greater understanding of ecology, economics and sociology as sciences in relation to the natural environment. And importantly we need to know the interactions and limitations of their basic factors, appraised and applied on the ground in practical terms.

In relation to all aspects of these sciences and the underlying forces and issues which are the subject of study, we need an effective predictive capacity. In this – as conservationists – we need constantly to have regard to the balance of resources available at any time – locally, nationally, internationally – and to make better forecast value judgements about the conservation planning, management and development of our natural environment. We can never lightly let current economic problems permit despoliation of the environment today and the jettisoning of adequate investment in science and planning for tomorrow.

The twin main themes of this meeting – the need for more understanding and the capacity for creative change – are therefore essential if nature conservation is to become a meaningful concept abroad and if at home we really are to improve the quality of our environment.

Nature conservation for me has always been and is today more than ever before the indicator or litmus paper of man's impact on the natural environment. In today's jargon it is at the sharp end. Concern about wildlife and their habitats is for many people their conscience about the quality of our one biosphere and a recognition of their obligations to posterity.

I have, therefore, greatly welcomed this Royal Society Discussion Meeting. I hope that it will help us to mobilize new knowledge for the work we so urgently need – that is to consolidate our gains and to start now to develop the scientific basis for the opportunities and challenges facing each and every one of us.